Learn all the key facts with CGP!

Ever wondered what you *really* need to know for KS3 Geography? Well, wonder no more — just look inside this Knowledge Organiser!

We've condensed every topic down to the vital information, so you can be confident you're memorising all of the content you need.

But that's not all... Try CGP's KS3 Geography Knowledge Retriever — it's great for testing yourself on all the knowledge you've taken in.

CGP — still the best! ☺

Our sole aim here at CGP is to produce the highest quality books — carefully written, immaculately presented and dangerously close to being funny.

Then we work our socks off to get them out to you — at the cheapest possible prices.

Contents

Section 11 — Geographical Enquiry and Skills

Literacy rate data on pages 3-5 and 51: UNESCO Institute for Statistics (uis.unesco.org). Data as of September 2021.*

Birth rate, death rate, life expectancy and total population data on pages 3-7, 51, 54 and 56, and distribution of wealth data on page 38: (1) United Nations Population Division. World Population Prospects: 2019 Revision, or derived from male and female life expectancy at birth from sources such as: (2) Census reports and other statistical publications from national statistical offices, (3) Eurostat: Demographic Statistics, (4) United Nations Statistical Division. Population and Vital Statistics Report (various years), (5) U.S. Census Bureau: International Database, and (6) Secretariat of the Pacific Community: Statistics and Demography Programme.*

Employment data on pages 4, 5, 52 and 55: International Labour Organization, ILOSTAT database. Data retrieved on January 29, 2021.*

Urban area population data on page 5 and 51: United Nations Population Division. World Urbanization Prospects: 2018 Revision.

Literacy rate data on pages 6 and 7, vegetation map on page 50, Lagos and Osaka population data on page 51 and 54, and population pyramid data on page 56: The World Factbook 2021. Washington, DC: Central Intelligence Agency, 2021. https://www.cia.gov/the-world-factbook/

Population under age 15 data on pages 6 and 51: World Bank staff estimates based on age/sex distributions of United Nations Population Division's World Population Prospects: 2019 Revision.*

Last 1000 years of climate change graph on page 17 reproduced with kind permission from the Intergovernmental Panel on Climate Change. Cambridge University Press.

Graph of World population growth 1500-2000 on page 32 from The World at Six Billion report by UN Population Division, © 1999 United Nations. Used with the permission of the United Nations.

Graph of World urban population 1950-2020 on page 35 from Annual Urban Population at Mid-Year, by UN Population Division, © 2018 United Nations. Used with the permission of the United Nations.

50 richest and 50 poorest countries data on page 38 and GDP data on page 55: World Bank national accounts data, and OECD National Accounts data files.*

Data used to produce pie charts on page 42: Feinstein, C H (1972), National income, output and expenditure of the United Kingdom 1855-1965, Cambridge: Cambridge University Press. Thomas, R and Dimsdale, N (2017) "A Millennium of UK Macroeconomic Data", Bank of England OBRA database: https://www.bankofengland.co.uk/-/media/boe/files/statistics/research-datasets/a-millennium-of-macroeconomic-data-for-the-uk.xlsx

Landsat imagery of Lagos, Nigeria on page 51 and of Osaka, Japan on page 54 courtesy of USGS/NASA Landsat.

*Licensed under CC BY-4.0. https://creativecommons.org/licenses/by/4.0/

Published by CGP.
Based on the classic CGP style created by Richard Parsons.

Editors: Ellen Burton, Katie Fernandez, Paul Jordin, Hannah Lawson and George Wright.
Contributors: Rosalind Browning, Paddy Gannon and Barbara Melbourne.

With thanks to Emma Clayton and Amy Turner for the proofreading.
With thanks to Alice Dent and Laura Jakubowski for the copyright research.

ISBN: 978 1 78908 925 7

Printed by Elanders Ltd, Newcastle upon Tyne.
Clipart from Corel®

Our World

Continents

CONTINENT — large mass of land and the islands closest to it.

Most countries are entirely part of one continent, but some are in two.

There are seven continents:

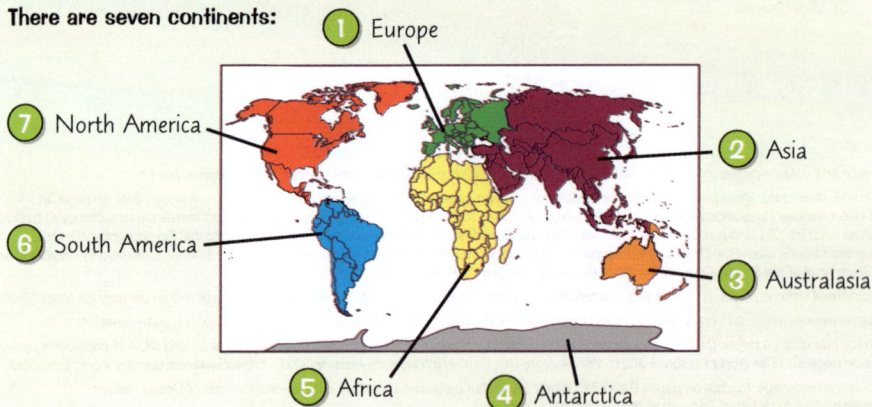

1. Europe
2. Asia
3. Australasia
4. Antarctica
5. Africa
6. South America
7. North America

Biomes

BIOME — area with a distinctive climate and vegetation.

Usually cover large areas spanning multiple countries.

Deciduous forest — broadleaf, e.g. oak. Coniferous forest — needles, e.g. pine.

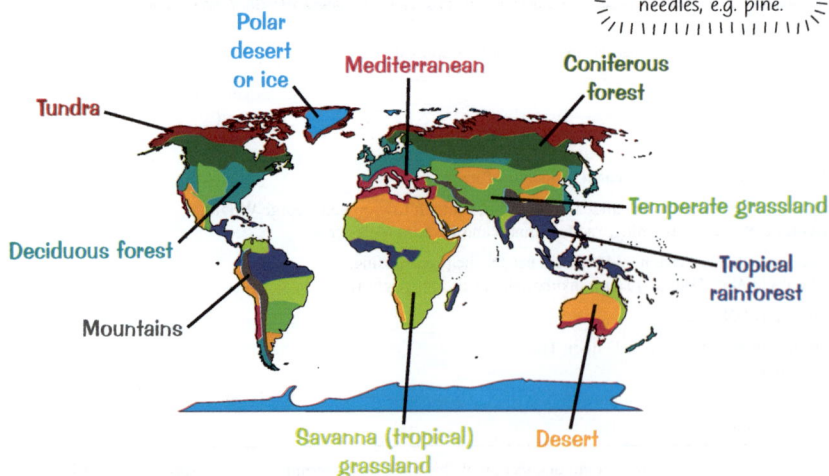

Polar desert or ice

Mediterranean

Coniferous forest

Tundra

Deciduous forest

Mountains

Temperate grassland

Tropical rainforest

Savanna (tropical) grassland

Desert

Africa

EXAMPLE

Map

AFRICA — a continent. It is made up of over 50 countries.

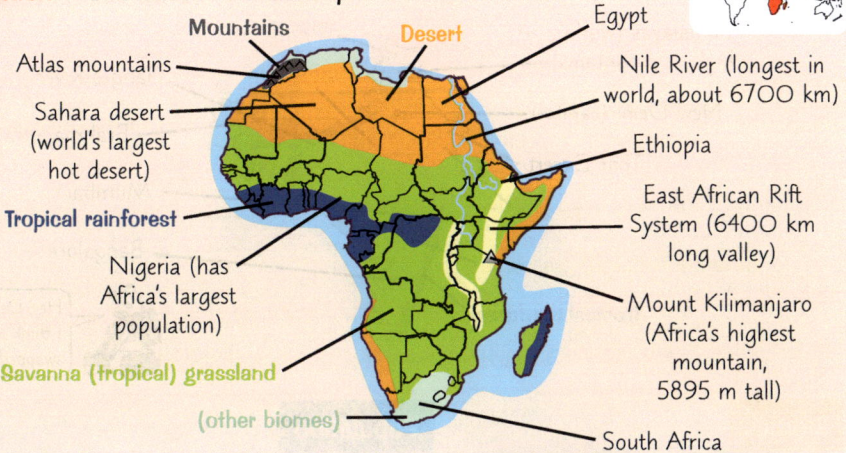

- Mountains
- Atlas mountains
- Sahara desert (world's largest hot desert)
- Desert
- Tropical rainforest
- Nigeria (has Africa's largest population)
- Savanna (tropical) grassland
- (other biomes)
- Egypt
- Nile River (longest in world, about 6700 km)
- Ethiopia
- East African Rift System (6400 km long valley)
- Mount Kilimanjaro (Africa's highest mountain, 5895 m tall)
- South Africa

Biomes

Most of northern Africa is hot desert:

Hot all year with very little rainfall.

Plants adapted for dry conditions, e.g. cacti:

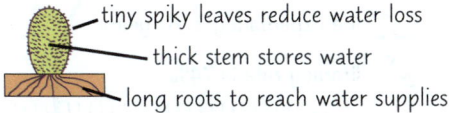

- tiny spiky leaves reduce water loss
- thick stem stores water
- long roots to reach water supplies

Most of rest of Africa is savanna (tropical) grassland:

Wet and dry seasons — warm all year but wet season warmest.

Plants have to survive dry seasons — e.g. grasses die down, trees have long roots.

Population

Second largest continent population — over 1.3 billion.

High birth rate — population is young and fast-growing.

Low density in deserts. High density where access to water — rivers, lakes, coast.

	Life expectancy	Literacy rate
Ethiopia	67 years (low)	52% (very low)
Egypt	72 years (quite low)	71% (quite low)

Economy

Many African countries have a low GNI per head. Farming is main source of food and income.

A few countries have a much higher GNI per head, e.g. due to tourism.

GROSS NATIONAL INCOME (GNI) — total value of goods and services produced by a country in a year.

GNI per head = GNI ÷ population

4

Asia — India

Map

INDIA — large country in south Asia.

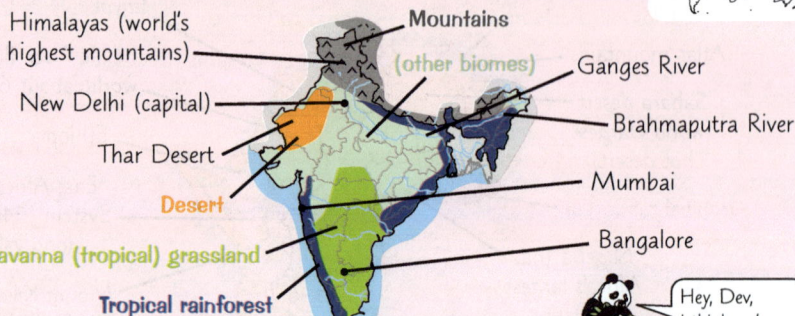

Himalayas (world's highest mountains)

New Delhi (capital)

Thar Desert

Desert

Savanna (tropical) grassland

Tropical rainforest

Mountains

(other biomes)

Ganges River

Brahmaputra River

Mumbai

Bangalore

Hey, Dev, I think we've swapped pages!

Biomes

Most of India has a tropical climate.

Some parts have a wet and a dry season — good for savannas.

Other parts are hot and wet all year — tropical rainforests:

Canopy layer — tall trees like mahogany.

Lower tree layer — smaller trees and climbing plants.

45 m

0 m

Not much undergrowth as trees block light.

Plants have waxy, pointed leaves which water runs off.

India used to have more rainforest — lots has been cleared for logs and grazing.

Population

India has a huge population (over 1.3 billion) which is young and growing.

Most people live in rural areas, but urban areas are growing rapidly as people migrate for jobs.

As a **NIC**, development level is between LEDCs and MEDCs:

life expectancy is 70 years

literacy rate is 74%

NIC = Newly Industrialised Country. Switching from farming to manufacturing/services.

Economy

Rapidly growing economy — 7th largest in world by GNI, although low GNI per head.

Wealth is unevenly distributed — many people can't afford good housing or sanitation.

Major sectors are farming and textiles — over 40% of people are dependent on agriculture for income.

Asia — China

EXAMPLE

Map

CHINA — large country in Asia.

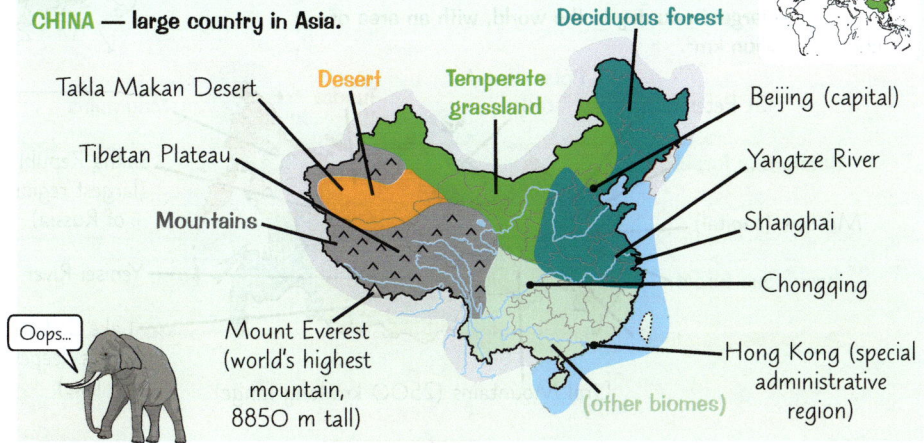

Deciduous forest

Takla Makan Desert

Desert

Temperate grassland

Beijing (capital)

Tibetan Plateau

Yangtze River

Mountains

Shanghai

Chongqing

Oops...

Mount Everest (world's highest mountain, 8850 m tall)

(other biomes)

Hong Kong (special administrative region)

Biomes

Main area of mountains is Tibetan Plateau:
- cold (warmer in valleys)
- not much precipitation
- short grasses adapted to dry, cold weather
- poor for crops — traditionally farmed by nomads herding livestock

Temperate grassland in central/northern China:
- cold winters and hot summers
- higher rainfall than Tibetan Plateau (mainly in spring/summer)
- good for taller grasses and cereal crops e.g. wheat

Deciduous forests in eastern China:
- milder winters, cooler summers
- highest rainfall

Population

Largest population in world (over 1.4 billion). Over 60% live in urban areas, with lots of migration to cities. Several cities have over 10 million people.

A NIC: life expectancy is 77 years

literacy rate is 97%

'One child policy': Introduced due to high pop. growth but ended 2016. Now lots more middle-aged than young people.

Economy

World's 2nd largest economy by GNI. Fairly high GNI per head.

Very large manufacturing industry — world's largest exporter.

Agriculture employs roughly a quarter of people.

Most business controlled by government until 1978, now many businesses privately owned.

Russia

EXAMPLE

Map

RUSSIA — largest country in the world, with an area of about 17 million km².

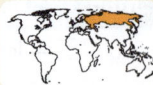

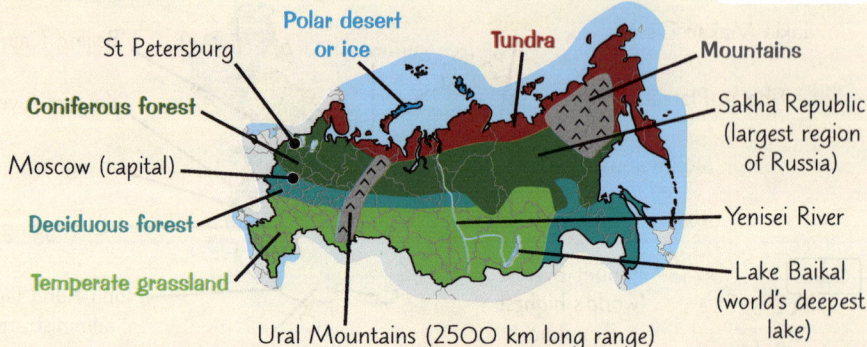

- St Petersburg
- Polar desert or ice
- Tundra
- Mountains
- Coniferous forest
- Sakha Republic (largest region of Russia)
- Moscow (capital)
- Yenisei River
- Deciduous forest
- Temperate grassland
- Lake Baikal (world's deepest lake)
- Ural Mountains (2500 km long range)

Biomes

Northern Russia — lots of tundra:

- **Very cold** — most ground is always below 0 °C (permafrost)
- **Little precipitation** — mainly as snow
- **Only small plants**, e.g. moss, lichen and grass
- **Polar desert** in far north — even drier and colder

Coniferous forest in central Russia:

- **Very cold winters and cool summers**
- **Inland so precipitation low**
- **Trees are coniferous:**
  Needles reduce water loss.
  Conical shape (snow slides off).
  Shallow roots so they don't freeze in ground.

Population

Population of Russia is about **144 million**.

Population **declined** in 1990s and 2000s, **grew** in early 2010s and **declining** since late 2010s.

Population is **ageing** — only 18% under 15.

Low population density — some large cities in west but large uninhabited areas in east.

Developed country: life expectancy is quite low (71 years)

literacy rate is very high (99.7%)

Economy

Russia has **large reserves** of raw materials:

- fossil fuels
- metals e.g. iron ore
- wood (world's biggest reserves)

Large **manufacturing** and **service** industries.

Moderate GNI per head but quite unevenly distributed — there are a few very wealthy people ('oligarchs').

The Middle East

Map

MIDDLE EAST — an area containing several countries
at the edge of Asia, Africa and Europe.

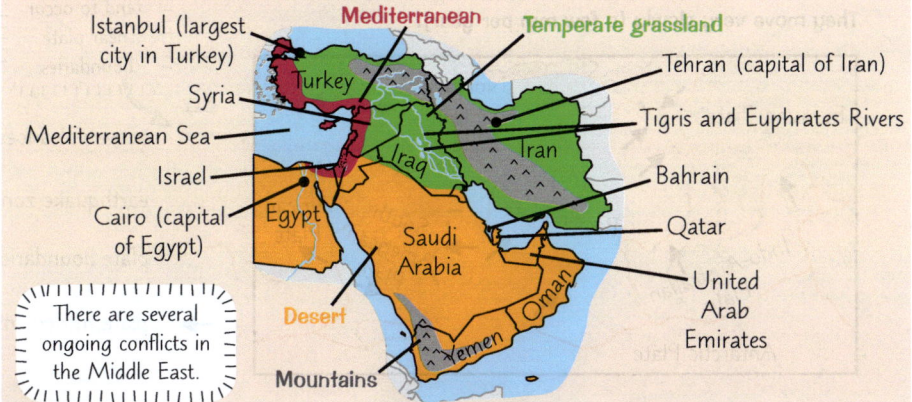

Istanbul (largest city in Turkey)
Syria
Mediterranean Sea
Israel
Cairo (capital of Egypt)
Mediterranean
Temperate grassland
Turkey
Iraq
Egypt
Iran
Saudi Arabia
Desert
Yemen
Oman
Mountains
Tehran (capital of Iran)
Tigris and Euphrates Rivers
Bahrain
Qatar
United Arab Emirates

There are several ongoing conflicts in the Middle East.

Biomes

Large parts of Middle East are hot desert — high temperatures and low precipitation.

Poor, sandy soil means not much grows — e.g. mainly small shrubs and herbs in Saudi Arabia.

Mediterranean biome around the coast of that sea:

Hot, dry summers and warm winters with some rainfall.

Evergreen and deciduous trees, thorny shrubs.

Population

	Examples
Size	Egypt largest — about 100 million Cyprus smallest — 1.2 million
Age	Iraq and Yemen youngest, Qatar oldest (as many adults move there for work)
Growth	Some countries affected by conflicts
Density	Very high in Bahrain, low in Oman
Distribution	Qatar mostly urban, Yemen rural
Literacy rate	High in Israel (98%), low in Yemen (70%)
Life expectancy	High in Israel (83 years), low in Yemen (66 years)

Economy

Many countries (e.g. Qatar) are wealthy due to large oil and gas exports.

There are other industries e.g. technology in Israel, agriculture and manufacturing in Turkey.

Conflicts can cause disruption to levels of development as well as loss of life. E.g. Iraq War, civil wars in Syria and Yemen.

The Tectonic Jigsaw

Earth's Crust

The Earth's crust is made up of plates that sit on top of the mantle.

Plates move due to convection currents in the mantle.
They move very slowly (a few mm per year).

Volcanoes and earthquakes tend to occur near plate boundaries.

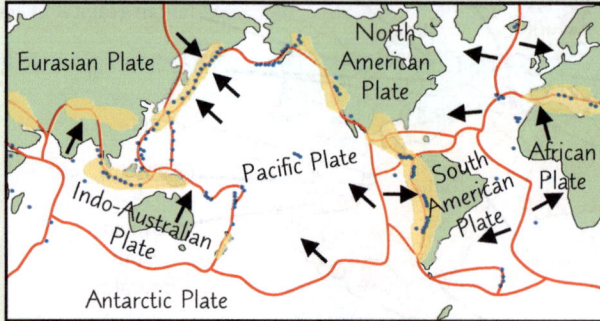

Key:
- •••• active volcanoes
- earthquake zones
- plate boundaries
- → plate movement

Eurasian Plate, North American Plate, Pacific Plate, Indo-Australian Plate, South American Plate, African Plate, Antarctic Plate

Three Types of Plate Boundary

1 Constructive
e.g. Mid-Atlantic Ridge

Volcanoes common.

Plates move away from each other.

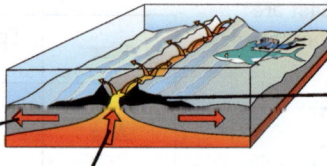

Magma rises to fill the gap.

Magma cools to create new crust.

2 Destructive
e.g. west coast of South America

Earthquakes and volcanoes common.

Plates move towards each other.

One plate is forced down.

Plate buckles and sediments build up, forming fold mountains (e.g. the Andes).

Heat and pressure force magma to surface, forming volcanoes.

3 Conservative
e.g. San Andreas Fault, California

Earthquakes common.

Plates slide in opposite directions.

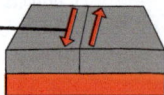

OR

SLOW   QUICK

Plates move in the same direction at different speeds.

Geological Time and Earthquakes

The Geological Timescale

GEOLOGICAL PERIOD — period of time when the formation of certain types of rock happened.

Earth's history is divided into geological periods.

Geological periods last for tens of millions of years — it takes a very long time for rocks to form.

Predicting Earthquakes

Hard to predict but some things give clues:

• changes to well water levels
• gas emissions
• cracks appearing in rocks
• unusual animal behaviour (maybe)

Earthquakes

Plate movement causes earthquakes. E.g. at destructive and conservative plate boundaries:

Plates get stuck as they move towards or past each other.

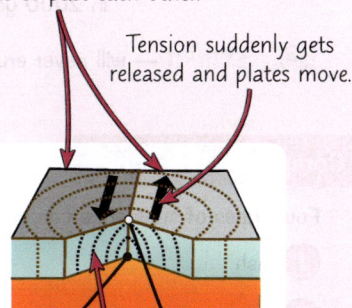

Tension suddenly gets released and plates move.

FOCUS — point where earthquake starts.

EPICENTRE — point on surface directly above focus.

Seismic waves spread out from focus. Most damage caused near epicentre.

The Richter Scale

Magnitude (size) of earthquake vibrations recorded using a seismometer. A seismometer records earthquake vibrations to produce a seismograph.

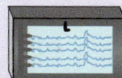

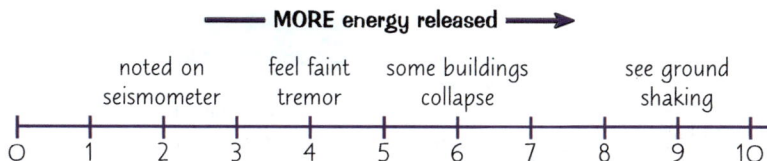

➤ **MORE energy released** ➤

noted on seismometer

feel faint tremor

some buildings collapse

see ground shaking

| 0 | 1 | 2 | 3 | 4 | 5 | 6 | 7 | 8 | 9 | 10 |

This is a logarithmic scale — e.g. magnitude 5 is ten times more powerful than magnitude 4.

buildings damaged

large buildings destroyed

most serious earthquakes that occur are in range of 5 to 9

Volcanoes

Volcanic Activity

Volcanoes can be:

ACTIVE — has erupted recently and likely to again.

DORMANT — hasn't erupted in **2000** years.

EXTINCT — will never erupt again.

Some signs that a volcano might erupt:

- lots of tiny earthquakes
- rising magma detected
- escaping gas
- hotter magma
- change in shape of volcano

Composite Volcanoes

Four types of substance can be ejected through vent:

1 ash

2 gas

3 pieces of rock (volcanic bombs)

4 molten rock

Molten rock is magma when it's underground and lava when it's above ground.

This material cools and hardens to form the volcanic mountain.

Mount Etna in Sicily is a composite volcano.

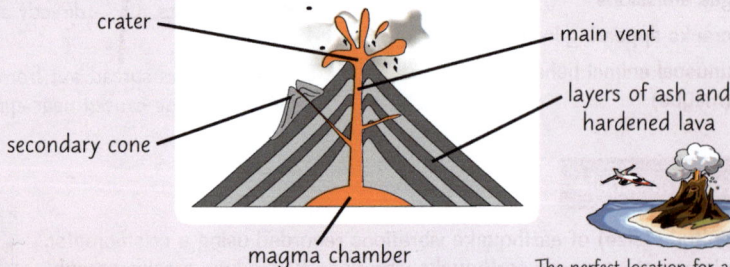

crater

main vent

layers of ash and hardened lava

secondary cone

magma chamber

The perfect location for an evil lair.

Shield Volcanoes

Mauna Loa in Hawaii is a shield volcano.

Made only of hardened lava.

wider and flatter

The lava is alkaline and runny so flows quickly and spreads out.

Lava Domes

Mount St. Helens (a composite volcano) has lava domes in its crater.

Made only of hardened lava.

steep-sided features

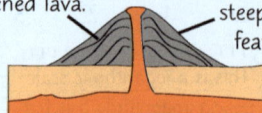

The lava is acidic and thick so flows slowly and hardens quickly.

Surviving Tectonic Hazards

Living in Hazardous Areas

Three advantages of volcanic zones:

1 Lava and ash make soil fertile.

2 Precious minerals present.

3 Hot water springs — good for heating and producing electricity.

Some people choose to live in earthquake or volcanic zones because:

• land is good for farming
• they feel safe there (e.g. with 'earthquake proof' houses)
• they want to stay (e.g. family has always lived there)

Sometimes people can't move away because:

• they can't afford to move
• there are too many people in zone to re-house everyone

Protection Against Earthquakes

Buildings and roads can be designed to cope with the strain of earth movements:

e.g. designing earthquake-resistant skyscrapers:

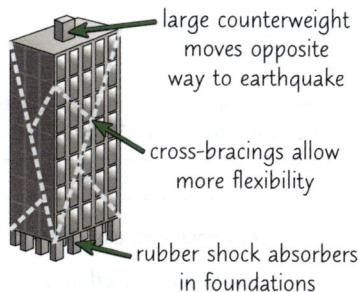

large counterweight moves opposite way to earthquake

cross-bracings allow more flexibility

rubber shock absorbers in foundations

Strengthening roads and railways can reduce damage, but doesn't always work.

Planning for Hazards

The effects of a hazard can be reduced by planning for them:

Authorities make disaster plans (e.g. how to get lots of people away from volcano).

Monitor early warning signs to predict when hazards are coming.

Prepare emergency services to deal with hazards.

Share information in schools, media, public meetings so people know what to do.

Families can prepare their own emergency supplies of essentials (e.g. water, food, spare clothes).

Prepare emergency supplies of water and power.

Tectonic Hazards in LEDCs and MEDCs

Three Factors that Affect a Disaster's Severity

1. **Rural/urban areas** — smaller disasters in rural areas, as fewer people and buildings.

2. **Population density** — the more people, the more deaths.

3. **Preparedness** — LEDCs have less time, money and expertise to prepare for disasters than MEDCs.

> MEDCs can't stop disasters happening, but they can limit the damage.

Emergency Plans

Countries can take action with emergency plans — to allow life to get back to normal after a disaster.

Organisation	Priorities
• get experts to assess situation • local citizens need info on what to do • individuals, government and NGOs need to be coordinated	• deal with immediate emergencies e.g. medical treatment, put out fires • fix power, water supply, sewers (risk of disease) • repair communication networks e.g. roads, bridges, railways, phones

Tectonic Hazards in LEDCs

LEDCs face barriers to carrying out emergency plans — it takes longer to get back to normal.

Preparation	Getting back to normal
• sometimes no plan due to lack of money and resources • poor communication so people don't know what to do	• limited facilities (e.g. hospitals, fire engines) — delays to dealing with immediate emergencies • badly-built housing more easily damaged so more fires and injuries • water/power supplies hard to fix • risk of disease outbreaks due to poor housing and limited medical facilities • takes time to bring in supplies — poor transport systems and reliant on foreign aid

Types of Rock

Two Types of Igneous Rock

	① Extrusive	② Intrusive
Example	basalt	granite
Texture	fine	coarse
Formation	Magma spills out onto the surface and cools there. magma chamber	Magma cools very slowly before reaching the surface.　Surrounding rock gets worn away. BATHOLITH — dome of cooled magma that is exposed by erosion.
Structures	When magma cools very slowly, large hexagonal columns form. E.g. the Giant's Causeway in Northern Ireland.	TORS — granite structures that have been worn down to leave large square blocks. E.g. the tors on Dartmoor.

Sedimentary Rocks

Formed from deposited particles.

Sandstones, shales and clays

Made from tiny particles of sand or clay eroded by wind or water and deposited in beds or strata, separated by bedding planes.

BEDS or STRATA — layers of rock.

Limestone and chalk

Made from remains of tiny shells and micro-skeletons — these are made of calcium carbonate, which reacts with dilute acid.

All rainwater is slightly acidic, so weathers limestone and chalk.

Coal

Made from carbon-rich remains of tropical plants.

Metamorphic Rocks

Two things that can change igneous or sedimentary rocks into metamorphic rocks:

① Heat from magma

② Pressure from earth movements

The chemical composition stays the same, but the rocks become harder and more compact.

Metamorphic rock formation:

Sandstone ⟶ Quartzite

Clays ⟶ Slate

Limestone ⟶ Marble

Granite ⟶ Gneiss

Weathering

Two Types of Physical Weathering

WEATHERING — breakdown of rocks by physical, chemical or biological processes. No movement involved.

1 Freeze-thaw

1. Water gets trapped in cracks in the rock.

2. Water expands when it freezes at night, putting pressure on the rock.

3. In the day, the ice melts and contracts, releasing the pressure.

FROST SHATTERING — alternating expansion and contraction weakens the rock and pieces break off.

2 Onion-skin

1. In the day, surface layers of rock heat up and expand.

2. At night, the cold makes them contract.

3. This causes thin layers to peel off.

Biological Weathering

There are three types:

1. **Plant roots** grow through cracks in rock surfaces and push them apart.

2. **Decaying plants/animals** make acids which eat away at rocks.

3. **Burrowing creatures**, e.g. rabbits and worms, break up softer rocks like clay.

Two Examples of Chemical Weathering

1 **Limestone** is dissolved by rainwater (a weak acid).

Dissolves along vertical weaknesses (joints) and horizontal weaknesses (bedding planes) — this creates special features called solution features.

E.g. in Malham in North Yorkshire.

2 **Granite** breaks down chemically to form kaolin or china clay.

E.g. in Cornwall.

Rocks, Landscapes and People

Chalk

e.g. South Downs

Quarried for cement and lime.

Chalk is porous so water soaks in — can be used as a natural reservoir.

Soil suitable for sheep farming and cereal crops.

Streams reappear at bottom of escarpment as springs — settlements tend to be near spring line.

Forms escarpments with gentle dip slopes and steep scarp slopes.

clay

Limestone

e.g. Yorkshire Dales

Quarried for lime, cement and building blocks.

Flat-topped moorlands with thin soil provide short grass for sheep farming.

Solution features:

KARST SCENERY — landscape produced by limestone.

limestone pavement with clints (blocks of limestone) and grikes (gaps between blocks)

swallow hole   stalactite   cave

scar

Water can't soak in but enters through joints (surface cracks).

Caves and gorges are tourist attractions.

bedding plane   stalagmite   clay

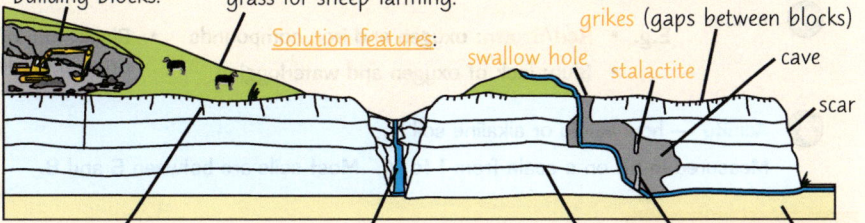

Granite

e.g. Dartmoor

Quarried for building material.

Dramatic features attract tourists.

Impermeable, so ideal for reservoirs.

Weathers to produce poor acidic soil: unsuitable for farming, suitable for, e.g. army training.

Resistant to erosion, forming distinctive tors and rocky outcrops.

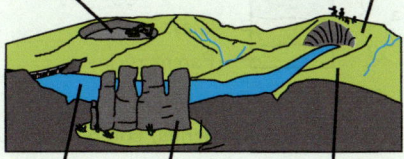

Quarries

Advantages:
- Provide building materials, cement and lime (used in fertilisers)
- Provide employment
- When quarrying stops, can be used as lakes for wildlife and sports

Disadvantages:
- Noisy and dusty, can be eyesores
- Increased traffic ⟹ air pollution
- When quarrying stops, often used as landfill sites

Section 3 — Rocks, Weathering and Soil

Soils

Five Components of Soil

1. **Minerals** from rocks, e.g. silt, clay and sand.

2. **Water** from rain.

3. **Air** in the gaps.

4. **Organic matter**, e.g. remains of dead plants/animals, decomposed material.

5. **Organisms**, e.g. woodlice, bacteria, worms.

Four Soil Characteristics

1. **Texture** — particle size.   E.g. sandy, clay, silt.

2. **Structure** — particle arrangement.   E.g. crumbly, blocky.

3. **Colour**
   E.g. • **Red/Brown**: oxygen and iron compounds
   • **Blue**: lack of oxygen and waterlogging
   • Black: lots of organic matter

4. **Acidity** — how acidic or alkaline soil is.
   Measured in pH on a scale from 1 to 14.   Most soils are between 5 and 8.

Soil Type Profiles

Temperate grassland soil
e.g. central Asia, central North America

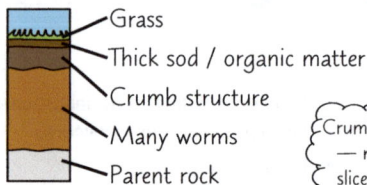

- Grass
- Thick sod / organic matter
- Crumb structure
- Many worms
- Parent rock

Crumb structure — not just a slice of toast.

Coniferous forest soil
e.g. north Asia, northern North America

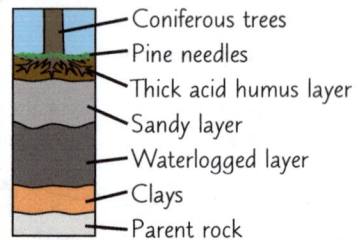

- Coniferous trees
- Pine needles
- Thick acid humus layer
- Sandy layer
- Waterlogged layer
- Clays
- Parent rock

Temperate deciduous forest soil
e.g. UK, western Europe, eastern USA

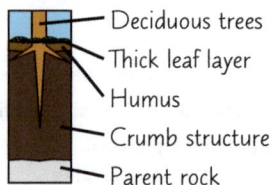

- Deciduous trees
- Thick leaf layer
- Humus
- Crumb structure
- Parent rock

HUMUS — decomposed organic matter.

Tropical rainforest soil
e.g. South America, south Asia

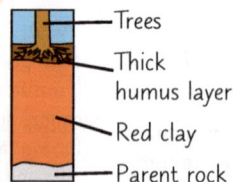

- Trees
- Thick humus layer
- Red clay
- Parent rock

Climate and Climate Changes

Climate and Global Temperature

CLIMATE — average weather conditions of a place.

CLIMATE CHANGE — any major change in weather of a region over long period of time.

Last **2.5 million** years: global climate shifted between...

- cold glacial periods (about 100 000 years)
- warmer interglacial periods (about 10 000 years)

20 000 years ago: Earth was cold (Ice Age).

12 000 years ago: end of last glacial period, Earth warms up.

Last **10 000** years: climate mainly warm.

Last **1000** years: climate fairly constant.

Last **100** years: global warming — rapid increase in global temperature (which scientists think is a result of human activities).

TIME

Earth is in an interglacial period now.

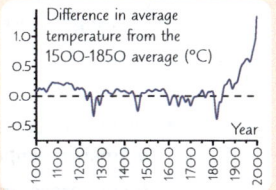

Difference in average temperature from the 1500-1850 average (°C)

World Climate Zones

Zones based on:

- maximum/minimum temperatures
- temperature range
- total precipitation
- seasonal distribution of precipitation

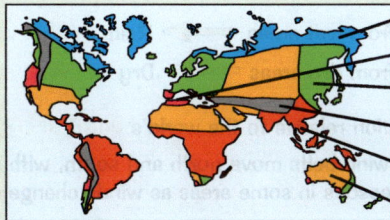

- Tundra
- Mediterranean
- Temperate
- Mountain
- Tropical
- Arid / Desert

Four Climate Graphs

Line graph shows temperature, bar chart shows precipitation.

1 Tropical

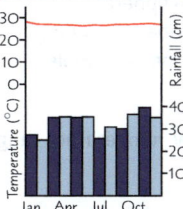

E.g. Amazonia

2 Tundra

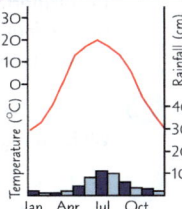

E.g. Siberia

3 Mediterranean

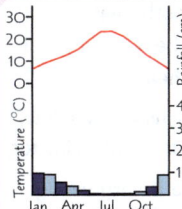

E.g. Spain

4 Tropical Monsoon

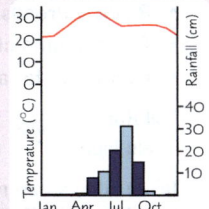

E.g. India

Climate and Microclimates

Five Factors Affecting Climate

1 **LATITUDE** — how far north or south of the equator a place is.

Further from equator $\Rightarrow$ Sun's angle is lower $\Rightarrow$ Overall temperature decreases

Temperature range over year increases

2 **ALTITUDE** — height above sea level.

Height increases $\Rightarrow$ Temperature decreases

Upland areas tend to be wetter too.

3 **DISTANCE FROM THE SEA**

- Places on or near coast have a smaller temperature range.
- Inland areas are drier.

Land heats up/cools down more quickly than the sea.

Wet winds from the sea lose their moisture before they reach there.

4 **PREVAILING WINDS** — usual direction of wind in a place.

Warm winds from hot areas $\Rightarrow$ Temperature increases

Cool winds from colder areas $\Rightarrow$ Temperature decreases

Winds from wet areas $\Rightarrow$ Rain

Winds from dry areas $\Rightarrow$ Dry

It's this way.

5 An area's position relative to the world's **WIND BELTS**

The six major wind belts move north and south, with overhead sun causing wet and dry seasons in some areas as winds change direction during year.

Urban Microclimates

MICROCLIMATE — climatic conditions specific to a small area.

Urban areas have higher average temperatures than rural surroundings:

- Buildings/roads absorb heat
- Air pollutants stop heat getting out
- Factories etc. add heat to air

Pollutant levels high $\Rightarrow$ Sunshine levels low, more cloud, rain, fog

Tall buildings can make it very windy (wind tunnel effect), or less windy (friction slows down air speed).

Four Factors Affecting Microclimates

1 **Surface Colour**
Dark: absorbs heat, light: reflects heat.

2 **Aspect**
In northern hemisphere:
South-facing slope $\Rightarrow$ sunny
North-facing slope $\Rightarrow$ cooler

3 **Water Areas**
Wet, windy, low temperature range.

4 **Surface Cover**
Bare surfaces — dry, windy, large temperature range.

Types of Weather

Five Weather Elements

	Measured using...	Recorded in...
1 TEMPERATURE — how hot or cold the air is.	thermometer	degrees Celsius (°C)
2 AIR PRESSURE — the force air exerts on an area due to its weight.	barometer	millibars (mb) Low — warm air rising High — cool air sinking
3 WIND — the movement of air from areas of high pressure to areas of low pressure.	wind vane (direction) anemometer (speed)	compass direction e.g. miles per hour (mph)
4 PRECIPITATION — all water that falls from clouds (e.g. rain, snow, hail, sleet).	rain gauge	millimetres (mm)
5 CLOUDS — water droplets suspended in the atmosphere.	(Can't be measured, can only be observed.)	(Type of cloud / amount of sky covered.)

Three Types of Rainfall

1 Relief

Rain shadow — drier area.

prevailing wind

1. Warm wet onshore winds rise over a mountain.
2. Air cools and condenses to form clouds. Rain starts.
3. Air reaches the summit and drier air descends.
4. Air becomes warmer and clouds evaporate.

2 Convectional

4. Condensation forms thick clouds.
3. Air cools.
1. Sun heats ground.
2. Hot air rises.
5. Heavy rain, sometimes thunder and lightning.

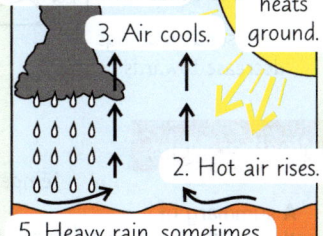

3 Frontal

FRONT — the boundary between two air masses of different temperatures.

cold front where cold air pushes warm air

warm front where warm air rises over denser, cold air

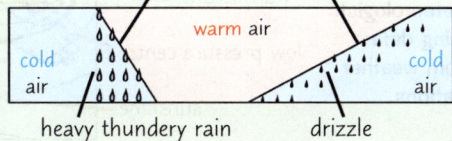

cold air
warm air
cold air

heavy thundery rain   drizzle

Weather Forecasting

Uses of Weather Forecasts

Things affected by weather need forecasts:

Transport: e.g. planes can't land in very high winds.

Sport: e.g. snow is needed for skiing, cricket is cancelled when it's raining.

Tourism: e.g. outdoor events may be cancelled if there is a storm.

Farming: e.g. some crops need harvesting in dry weather.

Energy production: e.g. wind turbines need wind, but can't be used in very high winds.

Pressure Systems

ISOBARS — lines joining points of equal pressure on a weather map.

HIGHS — areas of high pressure (also called anticyclones). Blue sky, sunshine.

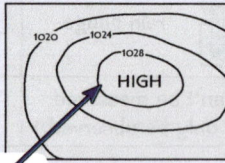

Isobar readings increase towards centre.

LOWS — areas of low pressure (also called depressions). Rain and wind.

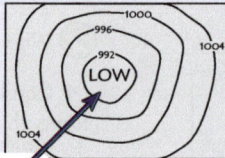

Isobar readings decrease towards centre.

Satellite Images

Images of clouds transmitted by satellites are used to predict weather.

Warm and cold fronts occur at edges of cloud formations.

Clouds circle low pressure areas.

Isobars follow cloud patterns.

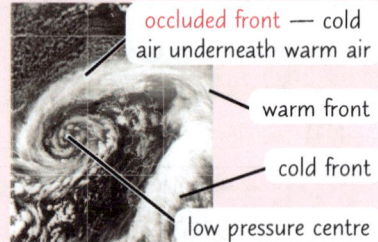

occluded front — cold air underneath warm air

warm front

cold front

low pressure centre

Infra-red images show temperature. Lighter colours — colder.

Weather Maps

A summary of the weather using standard symbols.

Produced by meteorologists using data from weather stations.

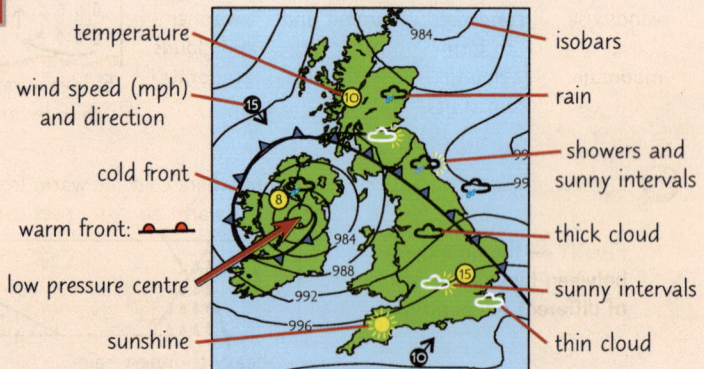

temperature
wind speed (mph) and direction
cold front
warm front:
low pressure centre
sunshine

isobars
rain
showers and sunny intervals
thick cloud
sunny intervals
thin cloud

The Hydrological Cycle

The Movement of Water

HYDROLOGICAL CYCLE — movement of constant amount of water between sea, land and atmosphere.

It has no start or end point.

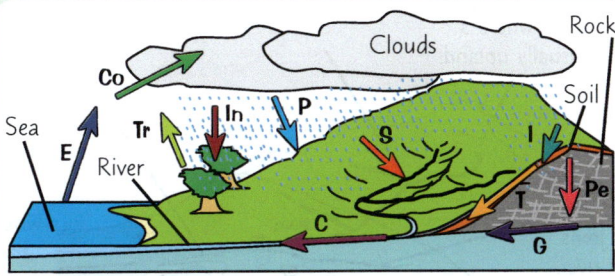

E: EVAPORATION
Sea, lake or river water is heated by sun and turns from liquid to water vapour (gas).

Co: CONDENSATION
Moist air rises and cools. Water vapour turns back into water droplets to form clouds.

EVAPOTRANSPIRATION
— evaporation and transpiration happening together.

P: PRECIPITATION
Rain, snow, hail or sleet falls from clouds.

S: SURFACE RUN-OFF
Water flows overground to rivers, lakes or the sea.

In: INTERCEPTION
Water collects on plants, before dripping off onto soil.

I: INFILTRATION
Water moves down through spaces in soil surface layers.

Tr: TRANSPIRATION
Plants lose moisture.

G: GROUNDWATER FLOW
Percolated water moves below the water table to a river.

T: THROUGH FLOW
Infiltrated water moves through soil to a river.

C: CHANNEL FLOW
Water flows in a stream or river.

Pe: PERCOLATION
Water moves deep into unsaturated ground until it reaches the water table.

Water table — upper surface of saturated rocks.

"Turn left at the salad bar and percolate until you reach the water table."

Four Water Stores

1. **CHANNEL STORAGE**
   E.g. in rivers and lakes.

2. **GROUNDWATER STORAGE**
   In porous underground rocks.

3. **SOIL MOISTURE STORAGE**
   In soil, used by plants.

4. **SHORT-TERM STORAGE**
   E.g. in plant leaves, flowers.

Drainage Basins

Features of Drainage Basins

DRAINAGE BASIN — land area from which a river and its tributaries collect precipitation.

Some basins are very large, e.g. the Amazon drainage basin covers most of Brazil.

SOURCE — where a river starts, usually upland.

CONFLUENCE — point where two rivers join.

MOUTH — where a river flows into sea.

TRIBUTARY — stream or smaller river that joins main river.

ESTUARY — where mouth is low enough to let sea enter at high tide.

Watersheds

WATERSHED — high ground separating different drainage basins.

Aerial View:

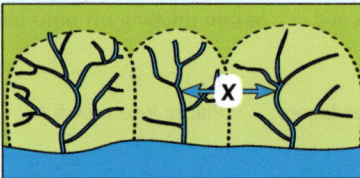

→ = movement of water drainage

- - - - - - = watershed

Section through X:

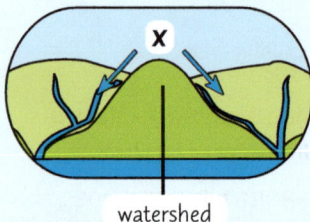

watershed

The Drainage Basin System

Water enters system as precipitation (e.g. rain, hail, sleet, snow).

Water can be stored in soil and vegetation before draining into river.

Energy is put into system by steepness of hills and force of gravity.

Water moves from high ground to the sea via rivers and below ground.

Time between rainfall and water entering sea varies with basin's characteristics, e.g. shape, size, rock type, vegetation.

Water moves rock/soil material through system. Picked up when energy is high, deposited when energy is low.

Rivers and Valleys

River Characteristics

DISCHARGE — amount of water that flows in a river per second.

River energy is linked to speed of flow. High speed = high energy, e.g. during floods, or when river gradient is steep.

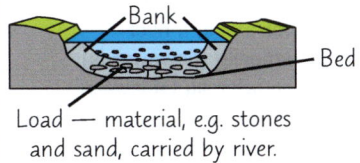

Bank

Bed

Load — material, e.g. stones and sand, carried by river.

Lots of energy ⟶ channel bed and banks worn away, producing load.

Little energy ⟶ load is deposited on bed and banks.

As river moves to sea: ↑ Channel width increases   ↑ Discharge increases

Three River Stages

	① Upper	② Middle	③ Lower	
Location	Near river's source	Lower down river	Near to sea	Sea
Long Profile	steep	gentle	very gentle (almost flat)	
Cross Profile (of river valley)	Narrow floor, steep sides (v-shaped).	Wider floor, gently sloping sides.	Wide floor, gentle sides (flood plain).	

Four Erosion Processes

① **ABRASION** — large pieces of load material wear away riverbed and banks.

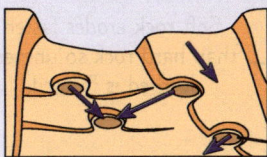

Material that collects in dips swirls around to form potholes.

➡ = water flow

② **ATTRITION** — rocks being transported knock against bed or each other and are eroded, becoming smaller and more rounded.

③ **HYDRAULIC ACTION** — force of water wears away at softer rocks (e.g. clay) or weakens rocks along bedding planes and joints.

④ **CORROSION** — when chalk and limestone dissolve in water.

Section 5 — Hydrology, Coasts and Glaciation

River Features

Interlocking Spurs

In its upper stage, a river erodes vertically (downwards) rather than laterally (sideways).

INTERLOCKING SPURS — ridges produced when a river twists and turns around hard rock along its pathway.

These ridges interlock like the teeth of a zip fastener.

Interlocking spurs, waterfalls and rapids are all found in the upper stage.

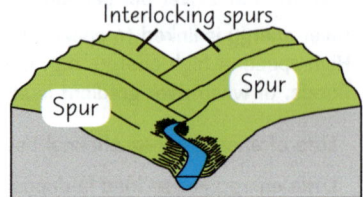

Interlocking spurs

Spur   Spur

V-shaped valley with interlocking spurs

Waterfalls

1. Layer of hard rock doesn't erode easily.

2. Softer rocks downstream are eroded more quickly, forming a waterfall.

4. Undercutting causes rocks to collapse, so waterfall's position retreats upstream and forms gorge.

3. Water wears away softer rock at foot of waterfall to form plunge pool.

Rapids

RAPIDS — series of little waterfalls.

Soft rock erodes faster than hard rock so uneven riverbed is formed.

Alternating bands of hard and soft rock

Section 5 — Hydrology, Coasts and Glaciation

River Features

Meanders

MEANDERS — series of large bends in rivers.

Current fastest on outside of curve, where channel is deeper.

Fast flow causes more erosion, forming river cliffs on outer edge.

Aerial View:

Cross-section:

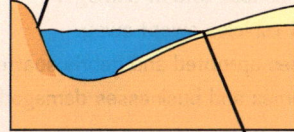

→ = strongest current

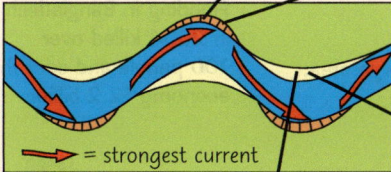

Inside of curve is shallow and current is slower.

Sandy material is deposited on inner edge to form point bars.

Ox-bow Lakes

Meander gets wavier over time until easiest path is straight across.

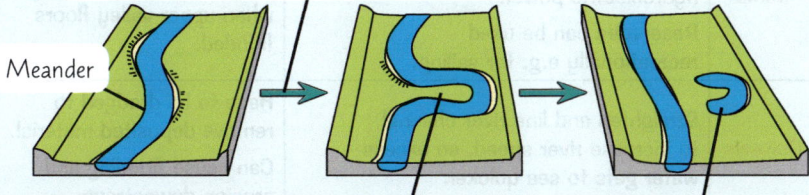

Meander

River breaks through narrow neck of land, usually when there is a flood.

Outer part of loop left isolated from river is an ox-bow lake.

Three Lower Stage Features

1. **FLOOD PLAINS** — wide valley floors which rivers regularly flood. Floods deposit fertile material on land, making plains good for farming.

2. **ESTUARIES** — the area of river mouths that are low enough that both the sea can flow in and the river can flow out.

3. **DELTAS** — features that form when river deposits its load too fast for sea to remove it, because either:
   - the sea is tideless (e.g. the Nile Delta)
   - the load is too big (e.g. the Ganges Delta).

Flooding

Boscastle, Cornwall 2004

EXAMPLE

Example of a flood in an MEDC.

Very high rainfall ➡ steep valleys and saturated ground meant water reached rivers quickly ➡ three rivers meeting meant lots of water at Boscastle.

Flood caused lots of damage:
- 115 vehicles swept away.
- Trees uprooted and debris scattered over large area.
- Homes and businesses damaged/destroyed.

Floods in LEDCs

Floods can be even worse in LEDCs as preparation, defence and recovery aren't as good.

Flooding in Bangladesh in 2004 killed over 700 people and cost the economy $2.2 billion.

Hard Engineering

Hard Engineering involves building structures to control the river system.

	Advantages	Disadvantages
Dams	Control discharge lower down the valley. Can be used to generate hydroelectric power. Reservoirs can be used recreationally e.g. for sailing.	Expensive to build. Farmland can be destroyed when upper valley floors flooded.
Culverts	Straighten and line river channel to increase river speed, so excess water gets to sea quicker.	Have to be dredged to remove deposited material. Can cause flooding and erosion downstream.

Other hard engineering strategies include:
- Increasing river channel capacity.
- Building branching channels off the main river to remove excess water.

Hard engineering structures can be ugly and disrupt river ecosystems. They can also cause a sudden disaster if they break.

Soft Engineering

Soft engineering involves changing land use to reduce flooding. Strategies include:

1. Afforestation (planting trees) on bare slopes to reduce run-off as trees intercept rain.

2. Having more plants/grass in urban areas to reduce amount of concrete, limiting rapid run-off.

Soft engineering used a lot in MEDCs where there's more money to invest in flood prediction, prevention and control.

The Power of the Sea

Wave Energy and Movement

Wave energy is determined by wave height and length, which vary according to:

- **Speed**
- **Length of time a wave has been moving**
- **Fetch** — distance of open sea over which the wind has blown

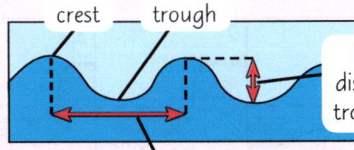

crest — trough

HEIGHT — distance between trough and crest.

LENGTH — distance between two crests.

SWASH — seawater moving up beach.

BACKWASH — seawater moving back to sea.

LONGSHORE DRIFT — when waves break at an oblique angle to shore (not at right angles) and push material along the beach.

Two Types of Wave

① Destructive	② Constructive
Operate in storm conditions.	Operate in calm weather.
Tall (can be several metres high).	Less tall (usually less than 1 metre).
Lots of erosion.	Limited erosion, lots of deposition.

weak swash / strong backwash

strong swash / weak backwash

Five Types of Coastal Erosion

1. **HYDRAULIC ACTION** — erosion caused by seawater crashing against land. Air and water get compressed in rock cracks. When sea moves away, the air expands, enlarging the cracks.

2. **ABRASION (or CORRASION)** — rock fragments batter land and cliffs, and break off other pieces of rock.

3. **ATTRITION** — rock fragments grind each other down into smoother pebbles, shingle and sand.

4. **CORROSION** — weak acids and salts in seawater can dissolve some rock types, e.g. limestone.

5. **WAVE POUNDING** — 'battering ram' action of weight of pounding waves.

Coastal Landforms

Landforms Caused by Erosion

CLIFFS:

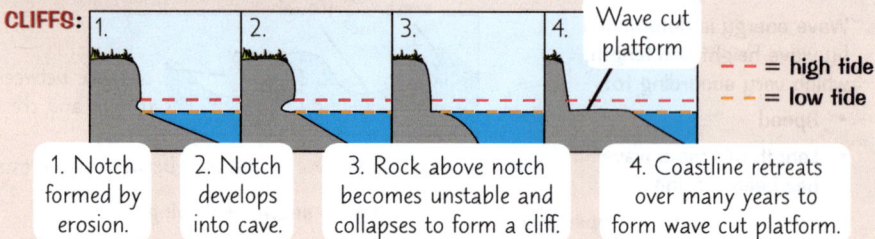

= high tide
= low tide

1. Notch formed by erosion.
2. Notch develops into cave.
3. Rock above notch becomes unstable and collapses to form a cliff.
4. Coastline retreats over many years to form wave cut platform.

HEADLANDS and **BAYS:**

Aerial View:

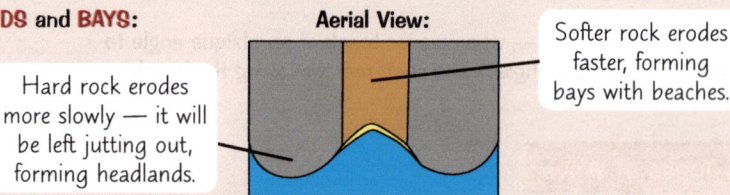

Hard rock erodes more slowly — it will be left jutting out, forming headlands.

Softer rock erodes faster, forming bays with beaches.

CAVES, **ARCHES** and **STACKS:**

Limestone or chalk geology prone to this erosion.

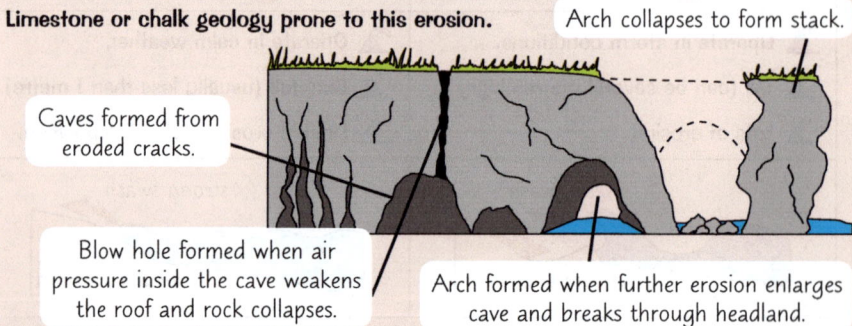

Arch collapses to form stack.

Caves formed from eroded cracks.

Blow hole formed when air pressure inside the cave weakens the roof and rock collapses.

Arch formed when further erosion enlarges cave and breaks through headland.

Landforms Caused by Deposition

BEACHES — found where eroded material in the sea has been deposited. Beach fragment size depends on local rock type and wave energy.

SPITS — long beaches sticking out to sea.

Longshore drift
River mouth
Spit
Marshy area

TOMBOLOS — ridges of deposited material formed between an island and mainland.

BARRIER BEACHES — where a spit has extended across a shallow bay. The water behind is left as a lagoon, which may slowly become a marsh.

The Coast and People

Coastal Protection

Ahh... finally no tourists.

Coastal areas are managed by national bodies or local authorities.

Coastlines can be fragile and easily damaged.

Protecting these areas can cause many conflicts:

Tourists want unrestricted access to coastlines.

Conservationists want to preserve habitats and protect wildlife.

Residents want to preserve their homes and livelihoods.

Coastal protection is very expensive — we can't protect everywhere.

> Coastal areas can be protected by reinforcing footpaths and fencing off at-risk areas.

Hard Engineering

HARD ENGINEERING — man-made structures built to defend coast from erosion and flooding.

Groynes: wooden structures at right angles to the coast.

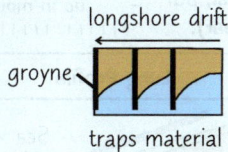

longshore drift

groyne

traps material

Sea walls: deflect waves to reduce erosion and flooding.

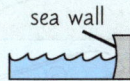

sea wall

Revetments: slanted barriers built when sea walls too expensive.

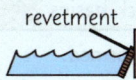

revetment

Gabions: steel mesh cages containing boulders that absorb wave energy, reducing erosion.

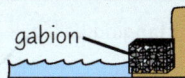

gabion

Armour blocks: large boulders piled on beaches.

rock armour

> These defences are ugly, expensive and not sustainable long term.

Soft Engineering

SOFT ENGINEERING — uses natural processes to slow erosion.

Beach nourishment: adding more sand to beach. Expensive and needs to be done again and again.

Shoreline vegetation: planting things like marshbeds to bind the beach sediment together.

Dune stabilisation: adding sediment and plants to dunes. Helps support the ecosystem.

Managed retreat: allowing erosion and moving buildings when needed. May be cheaper in the long term.

Set backs: building houses set back from the coast's edge.

The Work of Ice

Landscapes Shaped by Ice

Last glacial period started around 100 000 years ago and ended 12 000 years ago.

Glaciers ('rivers' of ice) formed and moved down valleys. Erosive power carved new features.

> Glaciated: covered in ice.

> Unglaciated: climate like modern tundra areas.

Three Actions of Ice

1 **FREEZE-THAW** — water freezes in rock cracks and expands, then thaws and contracts. Process repeats, which loosens surface and provides rock fragments for abrasion.

2 **ABRASION** — rock fragments in ice wear away rock which the ice is moving over.

3 **PLUCKING** (or **QUARRYING**) — meltwater at glacier base freezes on rock surface. Glacier moves forward, extracting pieces from rock.

Glaciers vs Rivers

Both start in highland areas and flow downhill, but glaciers are slower (3 to 300 metres per year).

> Glaciers start when snow and ice don't melt in summer, and ice builds up in mountain-top hollows.

Both have upland areas with erosion features and lowlands with depositional features (both can carry a solid load).

	Cross Profile	Long Profile	Contour Pattern
River		Sea	
Glacier		Glacier Snout	(after ice has melted)
	Rock basins		

Rivers flow to the sea, glaciers end in snout or sea.

Glacial Upland Features

CORRIE — steep-sided, armchair-shaped hollows with a lip at the valley end.

ARÊTE — knife-edged ridge formed when erosion narrows and steepens wall between two corries.

TARN — small lake in corrie.

Glacial Valley Features

Hanging valley

Truncated spur — ice cuts through spur leaving steep edges on valley side.

Waterfall

Powerful glacial erosion creates u-shaped valley.

Section 5 — Hydrology, Coasts and Glaciation

Population Distribution and Density

Where Many People Live

Areas with large populations tend to be accessible and have good resources.

Four types of densely-populated area:

1. River valleys — sheltered, river provides water and transport. E.g. Ganges Valley, India.

2. Lowland plains — flat so are accessible. Fertile soils allow productive farming. E.g. Denmark.

3. Coastal plains — ports good for trade and climate often moderate. E.g. New York, USA.

4. Areas with natural resources — provide raw materials (e.g. fossil fuels, ores) for industry. E.g. United Arab Emirates.

Where Few People Live

Three types of sparsely-populated area:

1. Hot deserts — high temperature and lack of water. E.g. Sahara Desert.

2. Very cold places — too cold for many plants to grow. E.g. Arctic Circle.

3. High altitudes — inaccessible and land hard to farm. E.g. Andes mountains.

Not sure what everyone's complaining about...

Population Density

POPULATION DENSITY — the average number of people living in an area.

$$\text{population density} = \frac{\text{number of people}}{\text{area}}$$

Figures for density must include units — usually people per km^2.

Density doesn't give the distribution of people inside an area.

Three Terms Describing Population Density

1. OVERPOPULATION — too many people to be supported by available resources.

2. UNDERPOPULATION — too few people to make the most of available resources.

3. OPTIMUM POPULATION — available resources can be used to best advantage without having too many people to maintain the standard of living.

Population Growth

World Population Growth

Three factors determining population growth:

1 **BIRTH RATE** — number of live babies born per 1000 people per year.

2 **DEATH RATE** — number of deaths per 1000 people per year.

3 **MIGRATION** — number of people moving in or out.

Graph shows world population growth from 1500-2000.

20th Century — population explosion due to big drop in death rate.

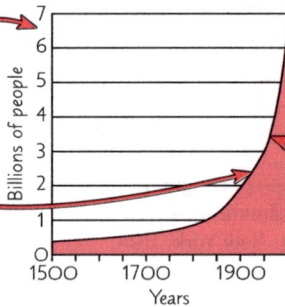

World population is growing rapidly.

Demographic Transition Model (DTM)

Natural increase: birth rate > death rate. Natural decrease: birth rate < death rate.

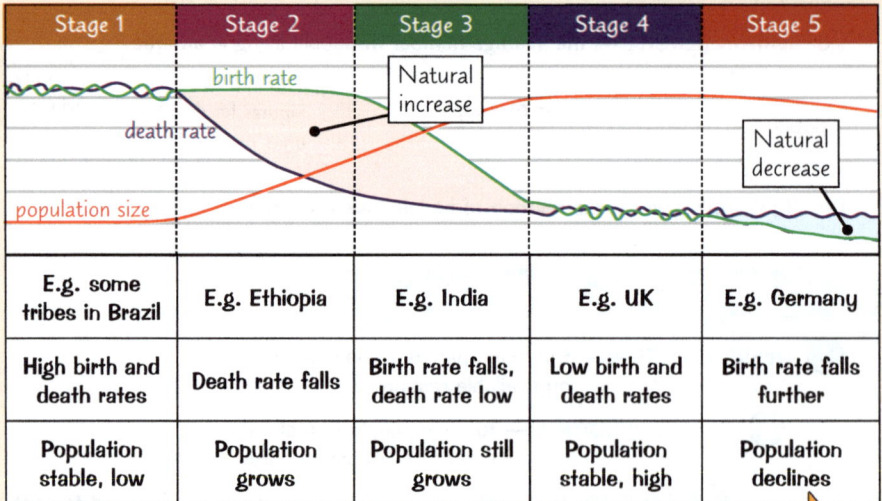

Economic development affects population growth.

Stage 1	Stage 2	Stage 3	Stage 4	Stage 5
birth rate death rate population size		Natural increase		Natural decrease
E.g. some tribes in Brazil	E.g. Ethiopia	E.g. India	E.g. UK	E.g. Germany
High birth and death rates	Death rate falls	Birth rate falls, death rate low	Low birth and death rates	Birth rate falls further
Population stable, low	Population grows	Population still grows	Population stable, high	Population declines

Stage 5 added to show recent population decline in some MEDCs.

Population Structure

Population Pyramids

POPULATION STRUCTURE — the number of males and females in different age groups. Shown by a population pyramid.

- Horizontal axis — percent of total population
- Vertical axis — age groups
- Left side — male population
- Right side — female population

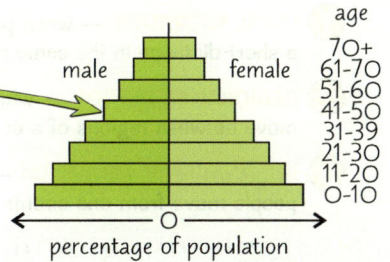

age
70+
61-70
51-60
41-50
31-39
21-30
11-20
0-10

male   female

percentage of population

Basic LEDC Population Pyramid

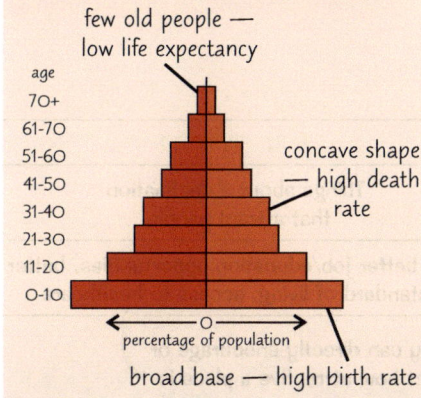

few old people — low life expectancy

concave shape — high death rate

broad base — high birth rate

age
70+
61-70
51-60
41-50
31-40
21-30
11-20
0-10

percentage of population

Basic MEDC Population Pyramid

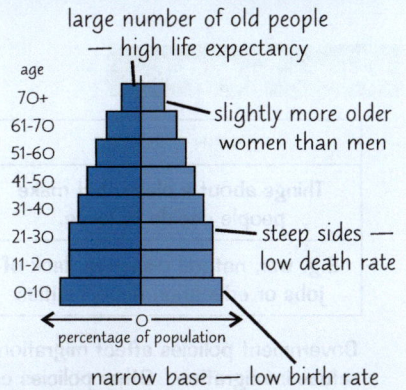

large number of old people — high life expectancy

slightly more older women than men

steep sides — low death rate

narrow base — low birth rate

age
70+
61-70
51-60
41-50
31-40
21-30
11-20
0-10

percentage of population

Three Variations of Population Pyramids

The new pyramid design was quite controversial...

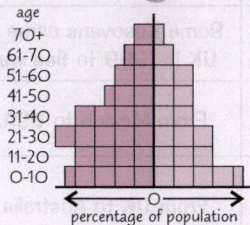

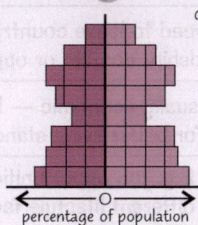

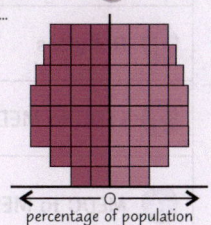

age
70+
61-70
51-60
41-50
31-40
21-30
11-20
0-10

① LEDC that has had high in-migration mainly by young men.

② Country that has had a war, followed by an increase in birth rate.

③ MEDC whose birth rate is so low, its population is declining.

percentage of population

34

Migration

Three Types of Migration

1 **LOCAL MIGRATION** — when people move a short distance in the same region.

2 **REGIONAL MIGRATION** — when people move between regions of a country.

3 **INTERNATIONAL MIGRATION** — when people move from one country to another.

International migration could mean moving across the world, or just a few miles over a border.

Three Key Terms

1. **MIGRANT** — person doing the moving.

2. **EMIGRANT** — person moving out of an area.

3. **IMMIGRANT** — person moving into an area.

Reasons for Migration

PUSH FACTORS	PULL FACTORS
Things about a place that make people decide to leave.	Things about a destination that attract people.
E.g. war, natural disasters, lack of jobs or education opportunities	E.g. better job/education opportunities, better standard of living, access to healthcare

Government policies affect migration — they can directly encourage or refuse immigration. Other policies can affect how attractive a place is.

Three Examples of International Migration

Migration	Reason	Example
1 Refugees	Forced to leave country due to hardship, conflict or oppression.	Some Kosovans came to UK in 1999 to flee war.
2 LEDC to MEDC	Usually economic — looking for better living standards.	From Mexico to USA.
3 MEDC to MEDC	E.g. job opportunities or different lifestyle factors (like warmer climate).	From UK to Australia.

When highly qualified people move abroad to better opportunities, it's called a 'brain drain'.

Urbanisation

Urbanisation Around the World

URBANISATION — growth in number of people living in urban areas.
Now over 50% of people in the world live in urban areas.

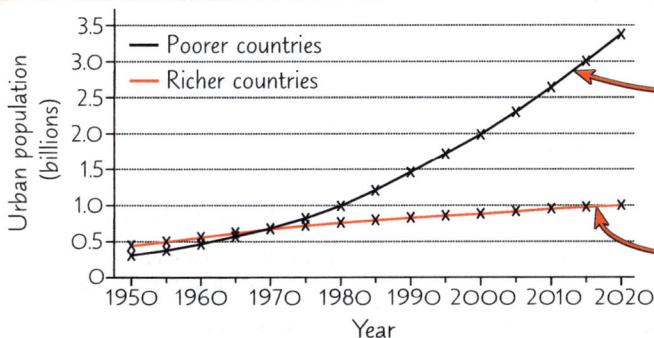

Most urbanisation is currently happening very quickly in poorer countries.

Most people in richer countries already live in urban areas.

Rural-Urban Migration

RURAL-URBAN MIGRATION — movement of people from countryside to towns and cities, causing urbanisation.

Has happened in **LEDCs** and **MEDCs** for different reasons:

LEDCs	MEDCs
• rural areas have poor access to services (e.g. water, power, education, healthcare) • urban areas seen as having better living standards • more jobs in urban areas • might be forced to move, e.g. by failing harvests	• in the past, new factories created jobs in urban areas • urban areas seen as attractive places to live, e.g. through redevelopment of run-down areas

Counter-Urbanisation

COUNTER-URBANISATION — movement out of cities to rural areas.

Counter-urbanisation occurs in MEDCs.

Reasons:
• rural areas seen as more relaxed than urban areas
• rural areas less polluted than urban areas
• may be able to live in rural area and commute to urban area

Urban Issues

Housing Shortages

Fast urban population growth ⟶ Urban housing shortages in some richer countries

Tackling housing shortages:

- Encourage investment to redevelop derelict areas, e.g. dockland development in Liverpool.
- Build new towns to house people from existing towns/cities, e.g. Milton Keynes in 1970s.
- Encourage people to relocate out of urban areas if they can, to make space for people who need it.

Oh, they're not hungry. They've just seen how much this nest would cost in the city.

Run-down CBDs

CENTRAL BUSINESS DISTRICT (CBD) — the part of an urban area where the shops and offices are.

Can be run-down because out-of-town shopping centres and business parks:
- have cheaper rent.
- are easier to drive to.

Four ways to make CBDs more attractive:
1. pedestrianise areas — safer and nicer for shoppers
2. improve access, e.g. public transport and parking
3. convert derelict warehouses/docks into new businesses
4. make public parks/squares nicer

Car Use

High car use in richer countries causes issues:
- More air pollution, damaging health and buildings
- More road accidents
- More traffic congestion

Four things that help reduce impacts of traffic in city centres:
1. alternatives to using cars — e.g. better public transport, cycle lanes
2. bus priority lanes to speed up bus services so more people use them
3. pedestrianised areas — no traffic and less pollution
4. parking charges to discourage car use

Ethnic Segregation

Cities are often diverse — people come from many different ethnic backgrounds.

But there can be ethnic segregation:
- people want to live close to people similar to themselves
- important services like places of worship might only be available in certain areas

Multicultural areas are supported by ensuring equal access to e.g. healthcare, education:
- make information available in different languages
- involve community representatives in decisions

Urban Issues

Squatter Settlements

SQUATTER SETTLEMENTS — housing built illegally in and around a city by people who can't afford proper housing (often rural-urban migrants).

Common in rapidly growing cities in poorer countries — e.g. São Paulo, Mumbai.

Living conditions can be very bad, with low life expectancy:

- often no clean water, sewers or electricity
- jobs involve long hours for little pay
- cramped houses made from waste
- lack of policing/medical services

Three ways to help improve squatter settlements:

1. Self-help schemes — e.g. government supplies materials then locals make improvements.
2. Site and service schemes — small rent charged to provide basic services.
3. Local authority schemes — local government provides funding to improve housing.

Waste Disposal

Three ways to deal with waste created by people in richer countries:

1. bury it in landfill
2. burn it
3. recycle it

Poorer countries struggle to deal with waste:

- Lack money to spend on safe waste disposal.
- Poor infrastructure — e.g. poor roads mean it's hard to collect rubbish.
- Rapid urbanisation means lots of waste every day so the problem is huge.

Air Pollution

Caused by factories, vehicle exhaust fumes and burning fuel.

Effects:

- Linked to some health problems, e.g. bronchitis.
- Causes acid rain which damages buildings and plants.
- Some pollutants damage ozone layer.

Water Pollution

Occurs when pollutants from cities get into rivers and streams.

Effects:

- Kills aquatic animals like fish.
- Toxins can build up through food chain and harm animals/humans.
- Contaminated water supplies spread diseases, e.g. typhoid.

Harder for poorer countries to manage pollution as dealing with it is expensive.

Measuring Development

Development

MEDCs — More Economically
Developed Countries (richer countries)

LEDCs — Less Economically
Developed Countries (poorer countries)

In 2017, the richest 50 countries had...	In 2017, the poorest 50 countries had...
62% of wealth	6% of wealth
15% of population	38% of population

DEVELOPMENT — how mature
a country's economy, infrastructure
and social systems are.
Higher level of development = richer.

North-South Divide

DEVELOPMENT GAP — contrast
between rich and poor countries.

MEDCs mainly in north —
moderate climate, good natural
resources, former colonisers

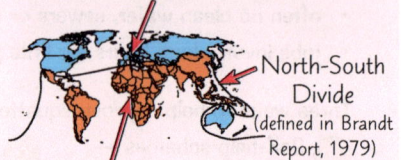

North-South
Divide
(defined in Brandt
Report, 1979)

LEDCs mainly in south —
more extreme weather/natural
disasters, former colonies

Eight Development Indicators

			Higher or lower in MEDCs?
1	GDP (gross domestic product)	Total value of goods and services produced per year — similar to GNI.	↑ higher
2	Life expectancy	Average age a person lives to.	↑ higher
3	Infant mortality rate	Number of babies who die under one year old, per 1000 live births.	↓ lower
4	Calorie intake	Average calories eaten per day.	↑ higher
5	Energy consumption	Average amount of energy used per person (indication of level of industry).	↑ higher
6	Urban population	Percentage living in towns or cities.	↑ higher
7	Literacy rate	Percentage of adults who can read.	↑ higher
8	People per doctor	Indication of access to healthcare.	↓ lower

Some indicators are linked, e.g. high
GDP and high urban population.

Two Problems with Development Indicators

1 Different indicators develop at different
rates and all figures are averages — no
measurement should be used on its own.

2 Information can be outdated or
inaccurate — some countries
can't measure it/won't publicise it.

Obstacles to Development

Natural Hazards

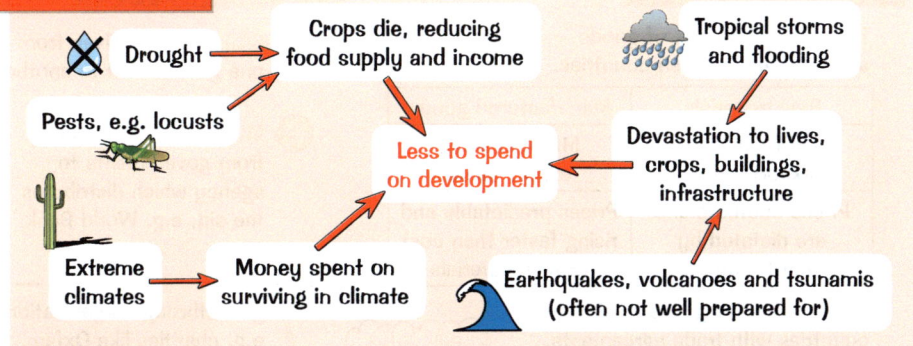

Drought → Crops die, reducing food supply and income

Pests, e.g. locusts

Tropical storms and flooding

Less to spend on development

Devastation to lives, crops, buildings, infrastructure

Extreme climates → Money spent on surviving in climate

Earthquakes, volcanoes and tsunamis (often not well prepared for)

Poor Health

Health problems in LEDCs use up a lot of the development budget:

➕ Poor diets — cause malnutrition and some diseases.

➕ Bad sanitation — water-borne diseases, e.g. typhoid, cholera.

➕ Malaria — tropical climate means mosquitos common in some LEDCs.

➕ High levels of STIs in some LEDCs, e.g. AIDS.

Colonial Period

The Developing World used to be colonies of European countries.

Colonies provided raw materials and agricultural produce and colonisers made colonies buy their goods.

Cotton produced in India bought by UK at low prices.

UK   India

Manufactured cloth sold back at a big profit.

Colonial pattern of trade still exists today:

- LEDCs produce raw materials (low value)
- MEDCs produce manufactured products (high value)

Debt

Many LEDCs borrowed money to finance development but became stuck in debt cycle:

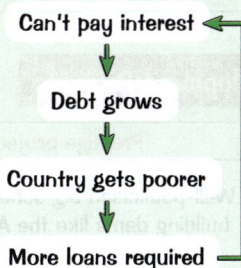

Can't pay interest

↓

Debt grows

↓

Country gets poorer

↓

More loans required

Cycle means many LEDCs can't invest in development.

Some debt cancelled by MEDCs, but most LEDCs have lots to pay back.

Trade, Aid and Development Projects

World Trade Patterns

TRADE — exchange of goods and services between countries.

Raw materials	Manufactured goods
LEDCs mainly export these	MEDCs mainly export these
Prices fluctuate and are dictated by MEDC buyers	Prices predictable and rising faster than cost of raw materials

TRADE BLOC — group of similar countries with trade agreements, including no tariffs. E.g. EU, NAFTA.

LEDCs not in a trade bloc can find it hard to export their goods.

Bella wished she hadn't learnt her trade technique on the playground.

Three Types of Aid

1 BILATERAL — given from one government to another.

2 MULTILATERAL — given from governments to agency which distributes the aid, e.g. World Bank.

3 NON-GOVERNMENTAL — given through organisations e.g. charities like Oxfam.

This type of aid is varied — can include small development projects and emergency help.

Arguments For and Against International Aid

For	Against
• Emergency aid saves lives in disasters. • Aid can help a country's economy develop by improving infrastructure. • Aid can help improve living standards, e.g. through clean water, better medicine, better food supply.	• LEDCs can become dependent on aid, so it can be used for political pressure. • Profits from aid projects might not stay in the country. • Aid might be used for prestige projects or kept by corrupt officials.

Development Projects

Prestige projects	Small-scale projects
Well-publicised big schemes — e.g. building dams like the Aswan Dam.	Specific improvements for a small area, e.g. creating infrastructure, providing a service, setting up co-operatives.
• Funding project causes large debts • Expertise provided by multinational companies — may take profits abroad • Might fail due to lack of infrastructure or correct equipment for maintenance	• Lower cost • Local people get training so they don't rely on outside help • Local people use local materials so doesn't require expensive maintenance

Industry

Four Types of Industry

1 **PRIMARY INDUSTRY** — involves collecting raw materials (anything naturally present in or on the Earth) in one of three ways:

- Quarrying, mining or drilling for below the Earth's surface (e.g. coal mining, oil drilling)
- Growing (e.g. farming, forestry)
- Collecting from the sea (e.g. fishing)

Adjo and Bakari out collecting the raw materials for tonight's dinner.

2 **SECONDARY INDUSTRY** — manufacturing a product. The finished product from one secondary industry may be starting material for another.

E.g. oil refining, fish processing.

One factory may make tyres which are then sent to be used in a car plant.

3 **TERTIARY INDUSTRY** — provides a service instead of making anything. The largest group of industries in MEDCs.

E.g. teaching, nursing, retail, police force, civil service...

It's possible to have, e.g. a tertiary job in a secondary industry.

4 **QUATERNARY INDUSTRY** — research and development.

Newest type of industry. Growing rapidly due to developments in information technology and communication.

Location of Industry

There are four big influences on the location of industry:

1 **Raw materials**
Being near raw materials reduces transport costs.
Ports used to import and export raw materials.

2 **Labour supply**
Unemployment varies by region.
Must be enough people with the right skills.

3 **Transport**
The cost of transporting raw materials and finished product.
The type of transport used (rail, road, air or sea).

4 **The market**
Being near where the product is sold reduces transport costs.
INDUSTRIAL AGGLOMERATION — concentration of linked industry in area.

Changing Industry in the UK

Two Reasons for Manufacturing Decline in the UK

1. **Natural resources running out** — many used up and others too expensive to keep extracting, e.g. tin mining in Cornwall. Some materials now imported from abroad.

2. **Competition** from countries that manufacture goods at cheaper costs. This is often due to lower wages, worse working conditions and less pollution control.

Many industries have relocated near ports or moved South.

UK employment in 1948 / UK employment in 2016

- primary
- secondary
- tertiary

Source: Thomas and Dimsdale (2017) derived from Feinstein (1972) and the Office for National Statistics.

Four Ways the British Government Affects Industry

1. Setting up industrial areas (trading estates) and Enterprise Zones to encourage new industrial and commercial businesses.
2. Encouraging companies to set up where there's high unemployment by giving incentives like cheap rent.
3. Encouraging development of derelict areas.
4. Encouraging foreign investment into the UK.

Growth of Footloose Industries

FOOTLOOSE INDUSTRIES — industries not tied to a raw material location. Locate in pleasant environments near transport routes and markets.

Science parks (e.g. Cambridge Science Park) are estates of modern, usually footloose industries, e.g. pharmaceuticals and computing, on the outskirts of towns.

There are three main reasons for their growth:

1. The need to be near research centres like universities.
2. Land is often cheaper on town outskirts and has better access to transport routes.
3. Information technology allows hi-tech industry to locate away from heavily populated areas.

Zara, you're so footloose.

Section 8 — Economic Activity and Natural Resources

The Use and Abuse of Resources

Using Resources

The world's resources are being used up quicker than ever because:

- economic activities use up natural resources,
  e.g. burning fossil fuels for electricity.
- the world's population is increasing so more resources are needed.
- standards of living are increasing for more people as countries develop,
  leading to increased consumption.

Sustainable resource use means meeting the needs of the present
without reducing ability of people in future to meet their needs. E.g. by:

Resource conservation   Pollution control   Resource substitution   Recycling

Energy Resources

NON-RENEWABLE RESOURCES
— resources of limited supply.
Fossil fuels (oil, coal and gas)
traditionally supplied most energy.

- Unsustainable (will run out).
- Major source of pollution.

Energy Debate Issues:

1. Balancing need for power and to
   protect environment.
2. Developing technology to improve
   alternative energy sources.
3. Making energy use more efficient.

RENEWABLE RESOURCES — won't run out.
These don't cause as much pollution.

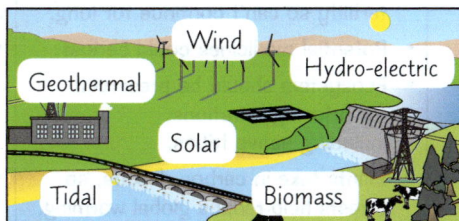
Wind, Geothermal, Hydro-electric, Solar, Tidal, Biomass

- Can be expensive.
- Need lots of space to produce as much
  energy as fossil fuel power stations.

Fishing

OVERFISHING — catching fish
more quickly than they can
reproduce. Depletes fish resources.

Fishing boats kill aquatic animals
by leaking oil into sea.

Quotas can help prevent
overfishing, but hard to enforce.

Fish farms prevent wild stocks
running out but can cause pollution.

Mining

Extracts useful resources e.g. metal, stone.	• Uses up natural resources. • Damages environment. • Can deplete water resources. • Can cause air, water and noise pollution.

Can be made more sustainable by reducing
pollution and restoring plant life in mined areas.

Section 8 — Economic Activity and Natural Resources

Deforestation and Conservation

Five Causes of Deforestation in Brazil

EXAMPLE

1 Trees logged and exported to MEDCs

Forest removal

5 Land flooded for hydro-electric power

2 Population increase — trees cleared for settlements

3 Cattle ranches

4 Mining — helps pay foreign debts

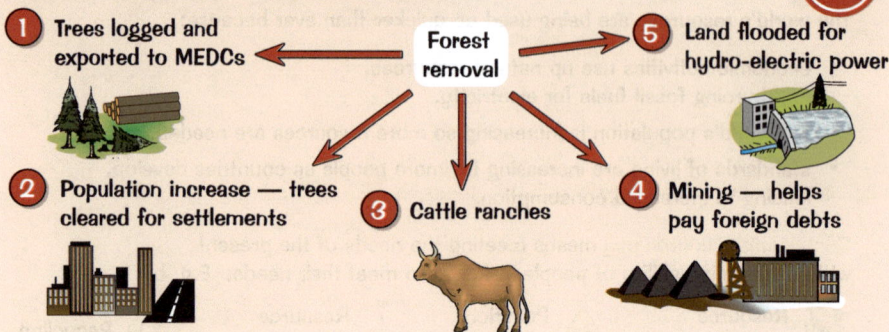

Deforestation Debate

For Conservation	For Deforestation
• Agriculture causes soils to lose fertility so can't continue for long. • Potential medicines could be lost. • Ecosystem should be preserved for future generations, including native tribes. • Plants take in carbon dioxide, so forests help reduce global warming. • Forest removal alters climate (e.g. caused drought in Ethiopia).	LEDCs should be allowed to chop down their forests because: • poverty means countries need to use all resources to help people. • many MEDCs destroyed their forests when developing. • most world carbon dioxide emissions don't come from LEDCs. • they might be trying to make money to pay debts owed to MEDCs.

Sustainable Forestry

Four techniques:

1 CABLING — pulling trees out using cables and winches.

2 REPLANTING — replacing trees that are cut down.

3 ZONING — identifying areas for different uses, e.g. national parks.

4 SELECTIVE LOGGING — only selected trees are chopped.

Preventing Bad Forestry

Promoting sustainable use of forests:
• creating demand for sustainable products and encouraging small projects
• encouraging ecotourism

Discouraging bad practice:
• preventing illegal logging
• banning unsustainable wood

Reducing need for deforestation:
• debt-for-nature swaps

Water Demand and Supply

In the UK

UK water companies try to balance water supply with demand.

Environment Agency in England and Scottish Environment Protection Agency in Scotland regulate water companies so that they act safely and sustainably.

More demand can mean shortages, so people have to save water.

 Hosepipe bans
 Water meters
 Fixing pipes
 Showers, not baths

Supply doesn't meet demand:

• Rain heaviest in north and west but more people in south and east.
• Rain heavier in winter but demand higher in summer.
   Storage and movement of water important, but expensive.

In LEDCs

Many LEDCs have serious water supply problems:

• Diseases such as cholera and dysentery spread through contaminated water.
• Demand for water increasing as countries develop and populations grow.
• Rainfall supplies can be unreliable and limited.
   Droughts can ruin crops and leave thousands without enough clean water.

Four ways LEDCs can improve water situation:

1 Farmers can use sprays or 'drip feeding' to water crops.

2 Self-help schemes can enable people to build simple wells.

3 Concrete lining of wells can reduce water loss.

4 Educating people about clean water and sanitation.

Well, well, well...

Aswan Dam — Egypt

EXAMPLE

The Aswan Dam on the Nile was built in the 1960s to help solve Egypt's water problems.

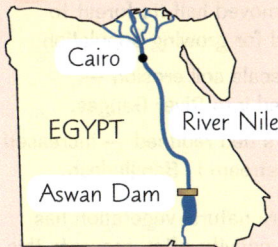
Cairo
EGYPT
River Nile
Aswan Dam

Advantages	Disadvantages
• Steady water levels. • Flood control possible. • Higher crop yields. • River can be used for transport all year. • Hydro-electric power.	• More Bilharzia snails that cause disease in humans. • Less sediment washed onto flood plains so more fertiliser needed. • Expensive to build. • Sediment will eventually fill reservoir.

Ecosystems

Food Chains

FOOD CHAINS — show what's eaten by what in an ecosystem.

Food for   Food for

Primary Producer —   Herbivore —   Carnivore —
green plant   eats the producers   eats the herbivores

PHOTOSYNTHESIS — how green plants use energy from sunlight to make their food.

$$carbon\ dioxide\ +\ water\ \xrightarrow{sunlight}\ sugar\ +\ oxygen$$

Nutrients return to soil when bacteria and fungi **decompose** dead organisms.

Humans depend on food chains for many things, e.g. food and medicines.

Carbon Cycle

Plants absorb CO_2

Respiration, burning, etc. releases CO_2

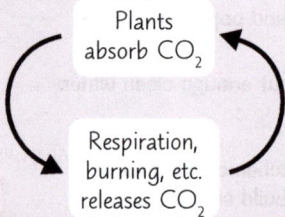

- Humans release huge amounts of CO_2 by burning fossil fuels.
- Deforestation reduces amount of CO_2 absorbed.

Nitrogen Cycle

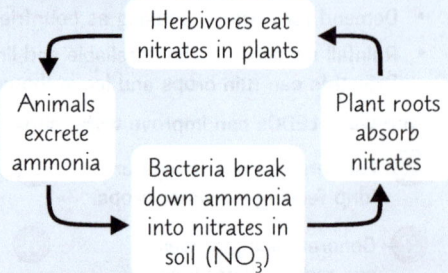

Herbivores eat nitrates in plants

Animals excrete ammonia

Bacteria break down ammonia into nitrates in soil (NO_3)

Plant roots absorb nitrates

Adding fertiliser to soil can alter nitrogen cycle and can cause algal blooms in water.

Human Effects on Ecosystems

UK — forest removed to make way for farms and settlements.

North America — grassland removed to grow cereal crops. Native Americans used to burn grassland to stop tree growth.

EXAMPLE

- From 1945-1985, Nepal (in the Himalayas) removed half its forest to make farmland for growing population.
- Caused large scale soil erosion — material washed into River Ganges.
- Depth of river's bed reduced — increased flooding downstream in Bangladesh.

Left alone, land develops into a **climax community** — where natural vegetation has developed fully (e.g. deciduous woodland in UK). Human activity often prevents this.

Acid Rain, Global Warming and Pollution

Acid Rain

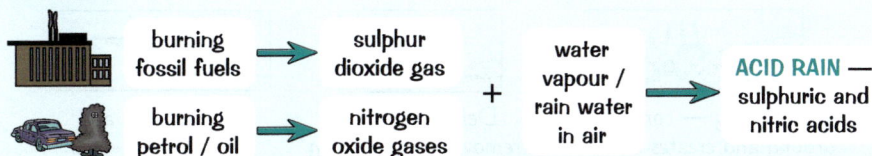

burning fossil fuels → sulphur dioxide gas

burning petrol / oil → nitrogen oxide gases

+ water vapour / rain water in air → ACID RAIN — sulphuric and nitric acids

Effects:
- Can kill trees and fish.
- Dissolves stonework of buildings.
- Increases leaching (removing nutrients from soils) — crop yields decrease.

Reduction:
- SO_2 removed from power station chimneys.
- Less burning of fossil fuels.
- Fitting catalytic converters to vehicle exhausts and limiting car use.

Global Warming

Burning fossil fuels releases carbon dioxide and methane into the atmosphere, increasing the greenhouse effect.

Heat trapped by CO_2

Energy from sun

Temperature rises

Effects:
- Ice sheets and glaciers melting, causing sea levels to rise — risk of flooding in low-lying areas.
- Freak weather e.g. storms, droughts.
- Change in world's climate.

- Britain and Europe have agreed to reduce greenhouse gas emissions.
- Some countries don't want to as could reduce rate of development / living standards.
- Oil states don't want to as oil sales will go down.

Four Types of Pollution

1. Air Pollution — created by burning fossil fuels and using agricultural chemicals.
2. River Pollution — from untreated sewage/waste, fertilisers and pesticides.
3. Sea Pollution — from industrial/household waste, oil spills and human sewage.
4. Land Pollution — from agricultural chemicals and industrial/household waste.

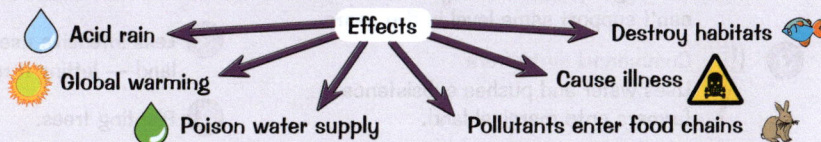

Acid rain ← Effects → Destroy habitats

Global warming

Poison water supply

Cause illness

Pollutants enter food chains

Section 9 — Influencing the Environment

48

Farming and Soil Erosion

Causes of Soil Erosion

Soil erosion happens when bare soil is washed or blown away.

Ploughing — compacts ground and creates channels for rapid water flow.

Deforestation — removes roots holding soil and allows wind and water damage.

Monoculture and fertiliser use — soil can't recover naturally.

Removal of hedgerows and windbreaks — wind erosion.

Overgrazing — vegetation removed faster than it can regrow.

Six Methods to Limit Soil Erosion

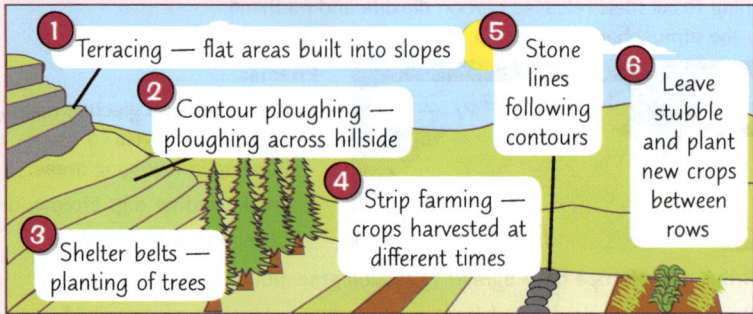

1 Terracing — flat areas built into slopes

2 Contour ploughing — ploughing across hillside

3 Shelter belts — planting of trees

4 Strip farming — crops harvested at different times

5 Stone lines following contours

6 Leave stubble and plant new crops between rows

These methods reduce run-off, minimise bare soil and protect from wind.

Desertification

DESERTIFICATION — when desert gradually spreads to surrounding areas, e.g. in central Africa.

Three causes:

1 **Population growth** More deforestation and farming — soil erosion.

2 **Climate fluctuations** Farming expands in wet years, but land can't support same level in dry years.

3 **Commercial agriculture** Uses water and pushes subsistence farmers onto marginal land.

Four solutions:

1 Minimising soil erosion.

2 Using branches instead of whole trees for fuel.

3 Less intensive use of land — letting it recover.

4 Planting trees.

Section 9 — Influencing the Environment

National Parks

Protected Areas

15 National Parks in Britain —
areas of natural beauty protected by law.

Much land privately owned and
many small permanent settlements.

Looked after by National Park Authorities who have three jobs:

1. Protecting the environment

2. Promoting enjoyment and understanding of parks

3. Looking after residents' interests

People go for outdoor activities and to enjoy nature.

■ = National Parks

Conflicts

Planning regulations very strict and development tightly controlled.

"You can't build here"

Industries in parks (e.g. quarrying) provide jobs but can destroy the landscape.

Tourists provide jobs and income but cause traffic, pollution and litter.

Visitors can damage farmland and animals, and cause footpath erosion.

PLEASE SHUT THE GATE

Honey-pots are areas that are very popular with tourists. They can become overused and lose their character.

- **Conflict resolution:** National Park Authorities resolve conflicts through public enquiries.
- Planning and development restrictions can control what goes on — e.g. park and ride schemes restrict vehicular access to parts of Peak District.

Section 9 — Influencing the Environment

Nigeria — Physical Geography

EXAMPLE

Location

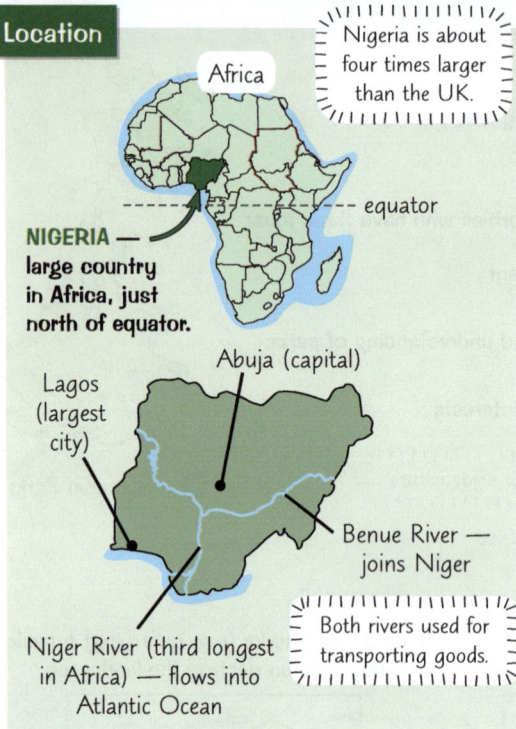

Africa

Nigeria is about four times larger than the UK.

- - - - - - - - - - - - - - - - - - equator

NIGERIA — large country in Africa, just north of equator.

Lagos (largest city)

Abuja (capital)

Benue River — joins Niger

Both rivers used for transporting goods.

Niger River (third longest in Africa) — flows into Atlantic Ocean

Biomes

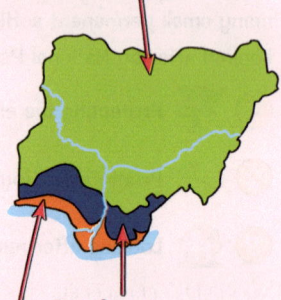

Most of inland Nigeria is savanna grassland. Precipitation lower than in coastal areas.

Rainforests grow in tropical climate. Some have been cleared for plantations/grazing.

Mangroves grow on tropical coast — trees here are adapted to live in salt water with strong roots rising above sea water.

Climate

Nigeria has a tropical climate — hot all year round and lots of precipitation.

The north of Nigeria is further inland — tends to be hotter and drier than south coast.

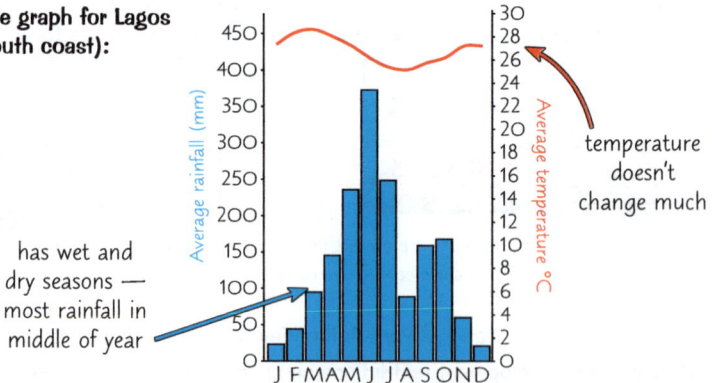

Climate graph for Lagos (on south coast):

Average rainfall (mm)

Average temperature °C

temperature doesn't change much

has wet and dry seasons — most rainfall in middle of year

J F M A M J J A S O N D

Nigeria — Population and Lagos

EXAMPLE

Development

Nigeria has a low level of development.

✏ Low literacy rate — about 62%.

〰 Education varies by region and gender — in some northern areas only a third of women are literate. 〰

🛒 Very high birth rate — 37 per 1000 people per year.

⚰ Death rate (11 per 1000 people per year) is much lower than birth rate so there is rapid population growth.

This also means the population is young — 43% are under 15.

Population Density

The south of Nigeria is much more densely populated than the north:

🛢 main oil and gas fields are in the south

🌳 south's rainforests good for crops (e.g. rubber, cocoa)

🚢 Atlantic coast is in south — has seaports and industry

Population Growth

About half the population live in urban areas.

This proportion is growing rapidly — people migrate to cities seeking better job opportunities/education.

Rapid growth has led to overcrowding in squatter settlements, and high numbers of unemployed people.

Lagos

LAGOS — huge urban area, Nigeria's main port. Population is 13 million to 21 million.

〰 The city started out on Lagos Island, but rapidly spread around edge of lagoon and onto other islands. 〰

Mainland

Lagos Lagoon — over 50 km long.

Atlantic Ocean

Lagos Island — where central business district is located.

USGS/NASA Landsat

Effects of rapid growth:
- Natural wetlands that helped prevent flooding were built on.
- Housing supply couldn't cope with growth — two thirds live in slums.
- High migration from rural areas has increased unemployment and numbers in 'informal' jobs (these aren't taxed or regulated).

Section 10 — A Study of Two Contrasting Regions

Nigeria — Economy

EXAMPLE

Employment

Division of labour in Nigeria:

A large percentage work in agriculture.

Most people work in services, e.g. retail, transport and financial services.

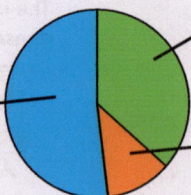

Industry employs a smaller proportion, but some industries (e.g. oil and gas) are very important.

Agriculture

About 35% of Nigerians work in agriculture.

Most are subsistence farmers — farm to feed their families.

Some work in commercial farming — i.e. for a profit.

Commercial crops (e.g. peanuts, cotton, rubber, palm oil) used to be big exports. Now oil is main export, but agriculture still an important sector of economy.

Oil Extraction

Important industry — oil makes up over 80% of exports.

Oil used to be even more dominant, but service sector has grown.

Industry held back by:

- inability to refine all oil produced (crude oil worth less than e.g. petrol)
- poor infrastructure
- damage caused by theft
- protests over pollution

Manufacturing

Nigeria's manufacturing industries are small considering its raw materials and large potential workforce.

Factors holding back manufacturing:	Government encourages manufacturing by:
• electricity demand exceeds supply — frequent power cuts • poor transport infrastructure leads to delays and high costs	• improving electricity generation • offering foreign companies incentives to build factories in Nigeria

High production costs caused Michelin to close its tyre factory in 2007 — even though Nigeria produces lots of rubber.

Section 10 — A Study of Two Contrasting Regions

Japan — Physical Geography (EXAMPLE)

Location

JAPAN — country that is a collection of islands off the east coast of Asia.

Japan is about 50% bigger than the UK.

Most people live on the four main islands:

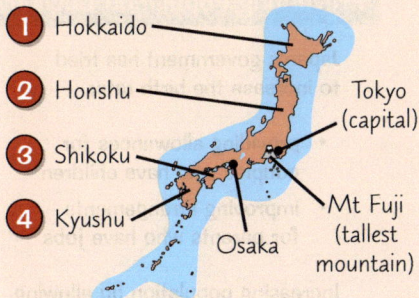

1. Hokkaido
2. Honshu
3. Shikoku
4. Kyushu

Tokyo (capital)

Osaka

Mt Fuji (tallest mountain)

Japan has over 6000 islands — most are uninhabited.

Terrain

About 80% of Japan is mountainous — urban areas concentrated on coastal plains.

Most rivers are short, steep and fast-flowing.

Varied vegetation:
- evergreen trees in south
- deciduous trees in north
- coniferous trees on high ground/in far north

Tectonic Hazards

Japan is close to boundary of several tectonic plates.

This makes the islands prone to earthquakes and tsunamis.

Many volcanoes — some are active.

Climate

Most of Japan has a temperate climate.

Climate graph for Osaka:

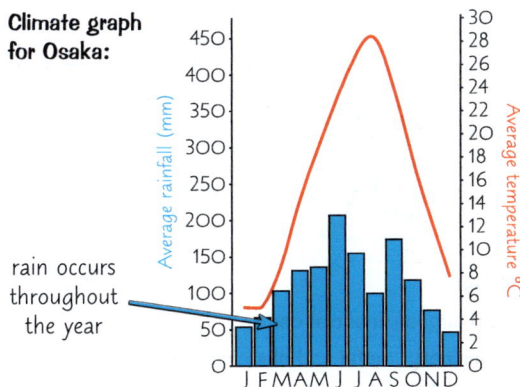

Average rainfall (mm)

Average temperature °C

rain occurs throughout the year

Far southern islands are warmer (subtropical) and far north is colder than rest of Japan.

temperature varies — winters are cool and summers are warm

JFMAMJJASOND

Section 10 — A Study of Two Contrasting Regions

EXAMPLE Japan — Population and Osaka

Development

Japan has a high level of development.

🖊 Very high literacy rate — over 99%.

🚼 Very low birth rate —
7 per 1000 people per year.

⚰ Death rate (11 per 1000 people per year) is higher than birth rate so the population is declining.

This means Japan's population is ageing (more old people than young people).

> Low birth rate as couples have fewer children to save money/ focus on careers. Low death rate due to good health care.

Population Density

🏢 Most people in Japan live in big cities with high population densities (e.g. Tokyo).

🚶 Rural population has declined due to migration — cities have more job opportunities and entertainment.

Preventing Population Decline

Japan's government has tried to increase the birth rate:

- providing allowances for couples who have children
- improving arrangements for parents who have jobs

Increasing population by allowing more immigration is unpopular in Japan, so immigration is restricted.

Osaka

OSAKA — third largest city in Japan, on south coast of Honshu.

Population of city is 2.7 million (whole metro area has 19 million people).

Kobe (neighbouring port city)

Yodo River Delta

Ports

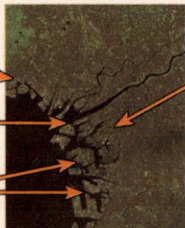

USGS/NASA Landsat

Osaka's inner city population is declining — people moving to suburbs or other cities.

> Most of Osaka is low-lying (some is reclaimed land on the delta) — vulnerable to flooding from typhoons or tsunamis.

Home to a variety of industries:

- Services — Japan's second largest financial centre
- Secondary industry — machinery, metal and chemical production
- Foreign trade — Osaka and Kobe make up Japan's biggest port

Japan — Economy

Employment

Division of labour in Japan:

Over 70% of people work in services, e.g. retail, finance and transport. Services generate most of Japan's income.

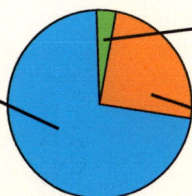

Relatively few work in agriculture.

The manufacturing industry is also a major part of Japan's economy.

Manufacturing

Manufacturing makes up about 20% of Japan's annual income.

Main manufacturing industries are a mix of traditional and high-tech:

Electronics and computers

Processed food

Pharmaceuticals (medical drugs)

Cars

Petrochemicals (e.g. plastics)

Metal production (e.g. copper and iron)

Much easier to clean up after.

Manufacturing industries have declined due to competition from cheaper foreign firms — especially traditional industries like ship building.

Agriculture

Farming — only about 1% of Japan's income.

Japan's mountainous terrain means large-scale farming is impossible.

Warm, wet climate suited to growing rice in irrigated fields.

About half of Japan's food is imported.

Research and Development

Research and development (quaternary sector) is important to manufacturing industry for creating high-tech products.

SONY® (Japanese electronics company) spends over £4 billion per year on research and development.

Comparing Nigeria and Japan

Population

Total population around 206 million, and growing rapidly.

Nigeria

Youthful population, with low life expectancy (55 years).

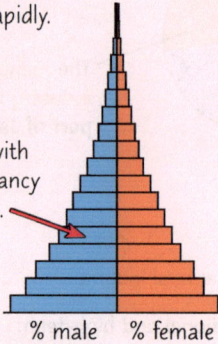

Japan

Total population around 126 million, and declining.

Ageing population, with high life expectancy (85 years).

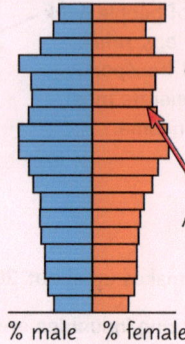

85+
80-84
75-79
70-74
65-69
60-64
55-59
50-54
45-49
40-44
35-39
30-34
25-29
20-24
15-19
10-14
5-9
0-4
age group

% male   % female

% male   % female

Data from 2020

Other Comparisons

	Nigeria	Japan
Location	• Northern hemisphere, near equator	• Northern hemisphere, further from equator
Climate	• Varied across country • Hot with lots of rainfall near coast • Hotter and drier inland	• Mostly one type of climate • Cooler than Nigeria, although southern areas have hot summers
Physical Geography	• Has several different environments, e.g. mangroves • Two long rivers flow through the country • Large areas are relatively flat	• Different vegetation to Nigeria — variety of types of tree • All rivers are short as no source far from sea • Very mountainous
Economy	• Most work in services or agriculture • Manufacturing growing slowly due to poor infrastructure	• Dominated by services • Few people employed in agriculture • Manufacturing slowly declining

Geographical Enquiry

Geographical Enquiry

GEOGRAPHICAL ENQUIRY — investigation of a geographical issue or problem.

Questioning ⟶ Information collection ⟶ Information presentation ⟶ Information analysis

Local Issue	Global Issue
e.g. traffic congestion	e.g. deforestation in the Amazon
Questions that might be asked:	Questions that might be asked:
• what is happening to traffic?	• what is happening to the rainforest?
• where are the main problems?	• where is the rainforest located?
• why is traffic a problem?	• why is the rainforest changing?
• who is affected by traffic?	• who is responsible for changes?
• how is the issue being dealt with?	• how can the issue be dealt with?

Sources of Information

PRIMARY DATA — information you collect yourself. Sources include:

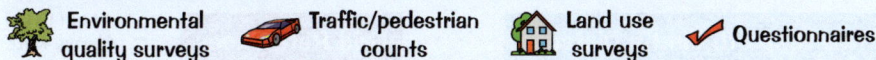

Environmental quality surveys   Traffic/pedestrian counts   Land use surveys   Questionnaires

SECONDARY DATA — information collected from another source. Sources include:

Newspapers   Websites   Books   Maps   The best sauce.

Using Sources

Analyse data to answer questions.

Websites	E.g. government websites have census data — information about population.
Maps	Show distributions. Can present land use survey data.
Statistical data	Can show trends over time. E.g. tally charts, pie charts.
Publicity leaflets	Usually show a range of different views and opinions, but can be biased.

Communicating Findings

Two ways to communicate findings:

1 Writing a report. Remember to:
• include both sides of story.
• give examples and sources.

2 Producing a leaflet.
• May include writing, photos, annotated maps, graphs and statistics.
• Should be tidy and presentable.

Reading Maps

Compass Points

Compass points can be combined, e.g. north-west.

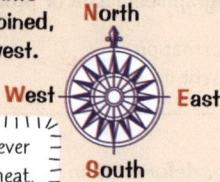

North

West — East

South

Remember: Never Eat Soggy Wheat.

Sketching Maps

Use a pencil.

Make sure shapes cross grid lines in the right place.

Get main shapes and road widths right.

Measure key points.

Contour Lines

You'd find these features on, for example, ORDNANCE SURVEY® maps.

CONTOUR LINES — lines that join points of equal height above sea-level.

Lots of lines ⟹ hilly or mountainous.   Lines closer together ⟹ steeper.

Few lines ⟹ flat, usually low-lying.   Lines further apart ⟹ flatter.

Spot heights show height of a particular place.

Top	Side
•456	

steep gentle

Top	Side
840	

steep gentle

Trigonometrical (trig) points show highest point in an area.

Height values are in metres.

Two Steps to Find a Distance

(1) Measure distance on map.

From church to church:

62

3.4 cm

0 cm 1 2 3 4 5

61

34   35   36

(2) Put ruler next to scale then read off the value on the scale.

Scale 1 : 50 000
2 cm to 1 km (one grid square)

2   1   0 km   1

0 cm 1 2 3 4 5

Make sure 0 is lined up with 3.4

Real life distance is 1.7 km.

Grid References

Always write Eastings first.

Four Figure:

- First two figures = Eastings (across) value for left edge of square.
- Last two figures = Northings (up) value for bottom edge of square.

48

P

47
88   89

P is at 8847.

48 0
9
8
7
6
5
4
3
2
47 1
0 1 2 3 4 5 6 7 8 9 0
88   89

P is at 885472.

Six Figure:

- Divide square into tenths.
- First three figures = Eastings value including number of tenths across.
- Last three figures = Northings value including number of tenths up.

Plans and Photos

Comparing Plans and Photos

Work out how photo matches plan by looking for main features. → E.g. lakes, big roads, woodland or railways.

Two types of question:

1 Name a place on a photo. → Match place names on plan to photo.

2 State what has changed between photo and plan. → Look at shapes to find out what has changed. Look at dates to work out which way round things have changed.

Town Plans

Small buildings = houses or shops.

Big buildings = likely factories or schools.

Lots of car parks and shops = CBD.

Group of houses surrounded by fields = village.

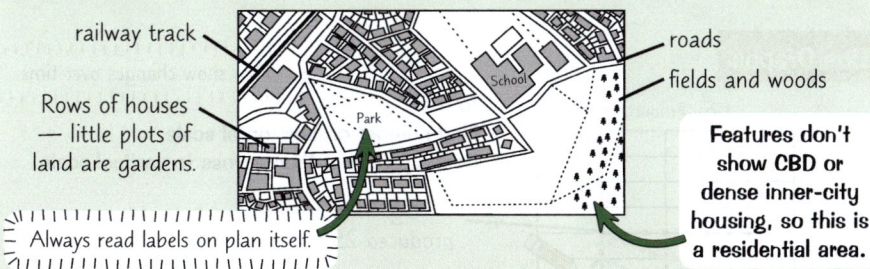

railway track →

roads

School

fields and woods

Rows of houses — little plots of land are gardens.

Park

Features don't show CBD or dense inner-city housing, so this is a residential area.

Always read labels on plan itself.

Aerial Photos

Look at aerial photos in same way as plan:

- what types of buildings,
- what kind of area it is,
- no labels, but might see cars and trees.

Tall buildings packed together (plus cathedral) = city centre.

Two Tips for Describing Photos

1 Check what the question asks:

"The photo shows a honey-pot..."

"List factors that attract tourists to honey-pot locations."

"List two factors that would attract tourists to this location."

Give everything you know about honey-pots.

Only list things you can see in photo.

2 Stick to things you can see in photo:

Physical geography, e.g. coastal and river features.

Human geography, e.g. building types, car parks, roads, paths.

Graphs and Charts

Bar Charts

Crude Oil Production

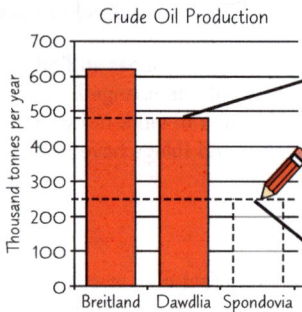

To read:
Find top of bar. Go to scale. Look at number.

E.g. Dawdlia produces 480 000 tonnes of oil per year.

To fill in:
Find number on vertical scale.
Trace line across to top of bar using ruler and sharp pencil. Use ruler to draw bar.

E.g. Spondovia produces 250 000 tonnes of oil per year.

Always draw bars same width as the others.

Line Graphs

Often show changes over time.

Coal Production

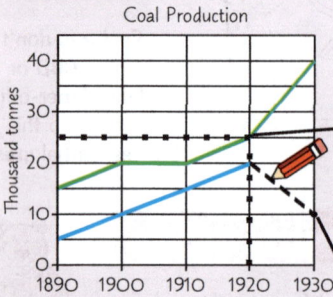

To read:
Find number on horizontal scale.
Read up to line, then across to vertical scale.

E.g. In 1920, New Wales Ltd. produced 25 thousand tonnes of coal.

To fill in:
Find number on horizontal scale. Go up to right value on vertical scale, and make mark. Join mark to line using ruler.

E.g. In 1930, Old Wales Ltd. produced 10 thousand tonnes of coal.

Pie Charts

To work out wedge %:
Write down where wedge starts and ends, then subtract.

To fill in:
Draw lines from centre to 0%, and outside number that you want. To do another wedge, add the % onto new start position.

Transport Type

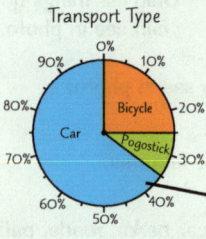

E.g. Car goes from 35% to 100%. 100 − 35 = 65%.

E.g. A new wedge of 20% ends on 45 + 20 = 65%.

E.g. This wedge is 45%.

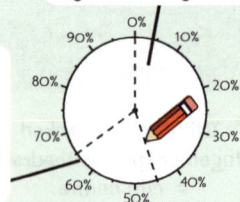

Section 11 — Geographical Enquiry and Skills

Graphs and Charts

Triangular Graphs

To read:

1. Find dot on graph. Turn graph so that one set of numbers is right way up. Follow line from dot straight across to number and write it down.

2. Repeat for each set of numbers.

3. Double-check numbers add up to 100%.

E.g. Population where 50% are aged under 30, 30% aged 30-60, and 20% aged over 60.

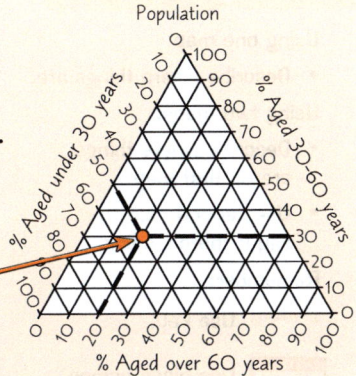

Population

% Aged under 30 years

% Aged 30-60 years

% Aged over 60 years

To fill in:

1. Start with one set of numbers the right way up. Find number you want, then draw faint pencil line across.

2. Do the same for other numbers, turning the graph each time.

3. Where three lines meet, draw a dot. Double-check by reading the numbers off.

Describing Line Graphs

Here are some things to look for:

Population of Downingham

Thousands of People

The peak (highest bit).

Where it's going down.

Where it's going up.

The trough (lowest bit).

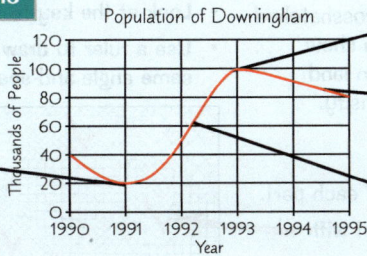

Scatter Graphs

Scatter graphs show correlation — how two pieces of data are connected together.

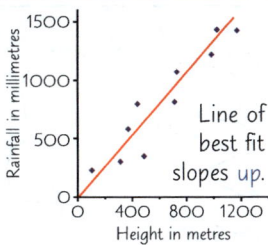

Rainfall in millimetres
Line of best fit slopes up.
Height in metres

Temperature in °C
Line of best fit slopes down.
Height in metres

Soil Acidity in pH
No line of best fit.
Height in metres

Positive correlation: height ↑, rainfall ↑.

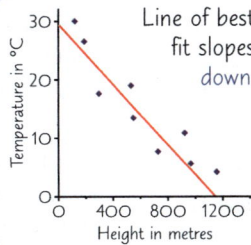

Negative correlation: height ↑, temperature ↓.

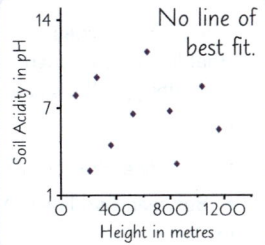

No correlation: height and soil acidity have no link.

Section 11 — Geographical Enquiry and Skills

Types of Map

Describing Distributions

Using one map:
- Describe where things are.

Using two maps:
- Describe where things are on first map.
- Use second map to say if there's a link.

Remember:

🗝 Use key.

HI MY NAME IS Use place names.

🧭 Use compass points.

Topological Maps

Topological maps show transport connections, often rail and underground networks.

Always read the key.

- Coast Line
- Cross Country Line
- Ferry
- Cable Car

lines crossing at a dot = place to switch between routes

dot = place

line = route between places

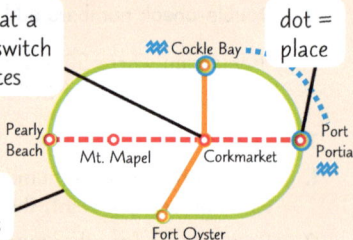

Cockle Bay
Pearly Beach
Mt. Mapel
Corkmarket
Port Portia
Fort Oyster

Choropleth Maps

Choropleth maps use crosshatched lines, dots or colours to show variation in areas, e.g. in land height or population density.

To describe:
- Look at the pattern of each part.
- Put a tick on each part with the pattern you want.
- Describe the parts with ticks on.

To complete:
- Look at the key to find the required pattern.
- Use a ruler to draw any lines, with the same angle and spacing as the key.

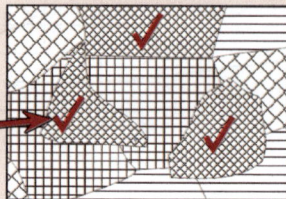

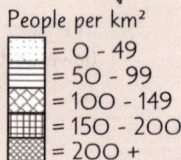

People per km²
= 0 - 49
= 50 - 99
= 100 - 149
= 150 - 200
= 200 +

Isolines

ISOLINES — lines that link places where something is the same.

E.g.
Contours = altitude.
Isobars = pressure.

To read:
- On a line → read off value.
- Between two lines → estimate.

To draw:
- Join dots with the same numbers.
- Never cross other isolines.

Rainfall on Thompson Island (mm per year)

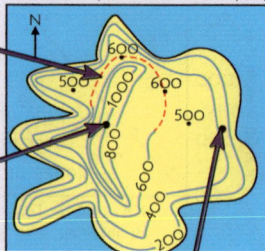

Points with 600 mm join up.

This point is on a line, so annual rainfall ≈ 1000 mm.

This point is midway between 200 mm and 400 mm, so annual rainfall ≈ 300 mm.

GNO31